Martin Gardner's Table Magic

Martin Gardner

DOVER PUBLICATIONS, INC.
Mineola, New York

Copyright

Published in Canada by General Publishing Company, Ltd., 30 Lesmill Road, Don Mills, Toronto, Ontario.

Bibliographical Note

This Dover edition, first published in 1998, includes selections from five books by Martin Gardner (*Match-ic,* Ireland Magic Company, Chicago, 1936; *12 Tricks with a Borrowed Deck,* Ireland Magic Company, Chicago, 1940; *After the Dessert,* Max Holden, New York, 1941; *Cut the Cards,* Max Holden, New York, 1942; and *Over the Coffee Cups,* Montandon Magic, Tulsa, Okla., 1949), and some new material.

Library of Congress Cataloging-in-Publication Data

Gardner, Martin, 1914–
    Martin Gardner's table magic / Martin Gardner.
       p. cm.
    ISBN 0-486-40403-X (pbk.)
    1. Magic tricks.   I. Title.
GV1547.G266   1998
793.8—dc21   98-28297
                                         CIP

Manufactured in the United States of America
Dover Publications, Inc., 31 East 2nd Street, Mineola, N.Y. 11501

CONTENTS

INTRODUCTION

The magic tricks in this book are selected from five books dating back to my youthful days in Chicago:

Match-ic (Ireland Magic Company, 1936), illustrated by Nelson Hahne.

12 Tricks with a Borrowed Deck (Ireland Magic Company, 1940), illustrated by Harlan Tarbell, introduction by Paul Rosini.

After the Dessert (Max Holden, 1941), illustrated by Nelson Hahne.

Cut the Cards (Max Holden, 1942), illustrated by Nelson Hahne.

Over the Coffee Cups (Montandon Magic, 1949), illustrated by the author.

For *Table Magic* I have reclassified the tricks into four categories: cards, matches, coins and bills, and impromptu table magic with common objects. Some new material has been added here and there.

Martin Gardner
Hendersonville, N.C., 1998

Part 1. CARDS

Although I have made every effort to eliminate unnecessary and difficult sleights from the tricks contained in this book, I have found that several of the effects require an ability on the part of the magician to execute the Erdnase in-jog shuffle for holding a top-stock of cards. Most card workers will be familiar with this shuffle, but for the benefit of those who are not (and who do not have a copy of Erdnase handy), it seemed advisable to include a description of how this shuffle is made.

The deck is held in the left hand, in readiness for an overhand shuffle. The back of the deck is on the thumb side of the hand. The right hand undercuts about three-fourths of the pack, and begins the shuffle. One card is run singly and in-jogged. This means that the card is pulled off by the left thumb in such a way that it projects slightly at the end of the deck nearest you. The rest of the cards are shuffled off on top of this jogged card. The right hand again undercuts about three-fourths of the pack. As the right hand takes these cards, the right thumb pushes in the jogged card and holds a break just *beneath* it. The cards are shuffled off until the break is reached, then the remaining cards are thrown on top. This completes the shuffle. It leaves the top quarter of the deck undisturbed.

With a little practice you will be able to execute the shuffle rapidly, with the card jogged only about a fourth of an inch, and the break held by the thumb made so small that it is almost indetectable, even to someone looking over your shoulder. I might add that after the card has been jogged, it is a good practice not to shuffle the rest of the cards flush with the pack. Instead, shuffle the cards flush with the jogged card at first, then gradually let the shuffle move forward. In this way the jogged card will not be obvious, and the break will be just as easy to obtain with the thumb.

The shuffle also provides a useful method of bringing a selected card to the top. Begin an overhand shuffle and continue until about half the cards are in the left hand. Have the card placed on top of this half. Then in-jog the next card and continue with the shuffle as described. At the conclusion of the shuffle the chosen card will be on top of the deck. To bring the card to a position of second, third, or fourth from the top it is only necessary to run the desired number of cards before making the in-jog.

The magician John Scarne preferred a variation of the Erdnase shuffle that was his own idea. Instead of in-jogging a card, he shuffled half the deck rapidly on top of the lower half, but jogged all of them *forward* slightly. The index finger of his left hand, curled around the front edge of the cards, prevented the lower half of the cards, and the forward jog of the top half, from being visible. He then simply gave the deck a cut by picking up the unjogged lower half and tossing them on top of the forward-jogged cards.

All of the card tricks in this book are, unless otherwise specified, original with me. Of course, many of them are merely a combination of fairly well-known principles or sleights.

IMPROVED TOPSY-TURVY DECK

The topsy-turvy deck principle, invented by Canadian magician Sid Lorraine, has had an interesting career. At the outset it was employed merely for a "flash" effect. The deck was apparently mixed so that half the cards, with their backs uppermost; were hopelessly intermingled with the other cards, which faced in the opposite direction. The performer explained that he was executing the "Slop Shuffle," the idea being that when the cards were later rearranged so that they all faced the same way again, the deck would be thoroughly shuffled. To prove that the shuffle was not quite so sloppy as it appeared, the magician tapped the deck on the corner, then spread it suddenly on the table. To everyone's surprise, the deck was exactly as it was before the shuffle had been made. It was not long until someone combined the "Slop Shuffle" with the discovery of a chosen card. The card was replaced, the "shuffle" was executed, then the cards were spread. The chosen card was revealed as the only face-up card in the deck. The use of one selected card soon led to the use of several selected cards. A riffle shuffle was employed to distribute the cards so that they would appear face-up in different portions of the spread.

In all of the above effects it was necessary for the performer to execute a "Half-Pass"—that is, to reverse secretly the lower half of the deck. In the method which I have worked out, this Half-Pass is eliminated. Three selected cards are handled. The procedure is clean, direct, and free from all suspicious moves.

Method

The trick works equally well with one, two, three, or more selected cards. We will assume that three cards are to be chosen. These cards must first be brought to the bottom of the deck.

Each performer will have his own method of bringing the cards to the bottom, but I prefer to employ what is known as the "Reversed Hindu Shuffle." The sleight was shown to me by John Snyder. I do not know who is responsible for its invention. It is not well known, and I may be the first person to put it in print.

The deck is fanned for the selection of three cards by three different people, then it is squared and held face down on the left palm. The right hand takes the end of the deck nearest you, and undercuts the cards. The well-known Hindu Shuffle is now made. This is done as follows. The right hand, with its half, is placed above the half in the left hand, and then withdrawn backward. As it is withdrawn, however, the left thumb and fingers press on the sides of the deck and retain a small packet of cards from the top of the upper half. After the upper half is withdrawn, this packet falls on top of the cards in the left hand. This move is repeated until the upper half is exhausted.

Hindu Shuffle the pack once. Begin the shuffle once more and continue until approximately three-quarters of the deck is in the left hand, then extend the left hand and ask the first person who selected a card to place that card on top of the cards in your left hand. Once that is done, place the cards in your right hand on top of those in your left, but hold the break with your left little finger. The tip of the finger should be between the two portions as if you were about to make the standard "pass." Now grasp the lower half of the deck with your right fingers and draw it backward. The little finger of the left hand presses on the selected card so that it is retained in the left hand, as shown in figure 1 (next page).

Immediately after the lower half has been withdrawn, leaving the selected card behind, the little finger is removed so that the selected card becomes the bottom card of the portion held by the left hand. Continue with the Hindu Shuffle until the cards in the right hand are exhausted. This leaves you with the deck in the left hand and the selected card on the bottom. At this point you apparently give the deck a quick cut. Actually you draw a portion of cards from the center and slap them on top. If the audience suspects that your shuffle brought the card to the top, this last move will throw them off the track.

The second selected card is handled in exactly the same manner. Undercut the deck about three-fourths, Hindu Shuffle two or three packets of cards, have the card replaced, and continue as just described. At the conclusion you will find both selected cards on the bottom of the deck!

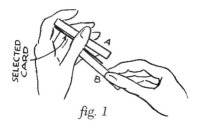

fig. 1

Any number of selected cards may be handled in this manner. A little practice is necessary to determine just how much pressure to apply on the card with the little finger. The pressure should be light rather than strong, otherwise it will retain more than one card. Watch your angles so that the little-finger break is concealed. I find it best to hold the cards to my left and tilted forward so that the backs are facing the audience and the cards are almost vertical. Then as the shuffle proceeds the cards may be brought forward again. The shuffle should be made rapidly, and the false cut executed at the conclusion.

After the three cards are brought to the bottom, it is necessary to crimp the cards slightly. Probably the simplest way to do this is to spring the cards from the right hand into the left. Another method is to riffle shuffle the cards (keeping the three on the bottom, of course) then conclude the shuffle with the familiar "waterfall" flourish which allows the dovetailed cards to fall back into place. This flourish will leave the cards crimped in the manner desired. The reason for the crimp will be made clear in a moment.

Now—execute the "Slop Shuffle." The deck is held in the left hand, back up. The left thumb pushes a small packet of about six or seven cards to the right. The right hand seizes this packet at the right edge, between the thumb and fingers. The thumb is on top. The packet is now turned over by rotating the cards toward yourself. At this point the left thumb pushes another small packet of cards to the right. This packet is picked up by the right hand. It goes beneath the cards already held in the right hand; that is, it goes under the right thumb. The right hand now turns these cards over again, this time rotating the cards forward. The left thumb pushes another group of cards to the right, and the right hand again picks them up. They are placed beneath the cards in the right hand, but since the right hand is in a different position, they go under the fingers instead of the thumb. These moves are now repeated. The right hand turns back and forth, picking up the packets after each turn, until there are no more cards in the left hand.

To the audience it appears exactly as if the cards are being hopelessly intermingled, some facing one way and some the other. Actually, at the conclusion of the "Slop Shuffle" you will find the deck divided into two parts. The upper half will consist of cards that are face up, and the lower half of cards that are face down. In short, the halves will be "back to back."

In employing the "Slop Shuffle" for this effect, the procedure is followed exactly as described, until about ten cards remain in the left hand. At this point the left thumb spreads the cards slightly and pushes to the right all the cards except the lower three. These three, it will be remembered, are the chosen cards. The right hand picks up all the cards in the left except these three, then turns the pack again, and the three cards are placed on top. It does not matter which side of the pack is upward, just that the three cards are placed face down on top of it.

It is a good plan to make the "Slop Shuffle" as sloppy as possible. That is, make no attempt to keep the cards neatly squared in the right hand. This will strengthen the impression that the cards are actually being mixed.

Square the cards and place them on the left palm as shown in the illustration.

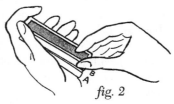

fig. 2

The three chosen cards are on top. Near the center of the deck there will be a break, produced by the previous crimping of the cards. The right hand takes the end of the deck nearest you (as shown above) and lifts off the upper half, cutting at the break. This half is placed on the table. The left hand follows, placing its half just to the left of the cards on the table, so that the cards are in a position to be riffle shuffled. As the left hand moves forward, however, it turns over, so that the portion it holds is placed on the table with the faces upward, as shown in figure 3.

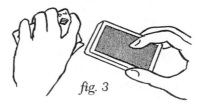

fig. 3

The right hand should place its half some distance forward on the table. All eyes will follow this motion. At this point, while the attention of the audience is misdirected, the left hand turns over, and comes forward to place its half on the table also.

It is this move that takes the place of the Half-Pass. The cards on the table are now all facing upward, with the exception of the three chosen cards, which are face down on top of the right-hand packet.

The inside corners of the two packets are riffled together. The riffling is done by the thumbs, with the backs of the hands covering as much of the two packs as possible. The riffling should be rapid, and well covered by the hands, as you do not wish the audience to see that the cards all face the same way. Before making the riffle, the right fingers slide the top selected card slightly backward, toward yourself. The right half is riffled more rapidly than the left, but the top card is retained by the right thumb so that it is the last card to fall in the shuffle. In other words, you riffle the right half rapidly, holding the top card, then finish riffling the left half, and finally drop the remaining card from the right hand. This is to make certain that the three selected cards do not remain together after the shuffle is completed.

After the riffle, push the halves together slowly, as the contrast between the face-up card on the left and the face-down card on the right strengthens the illusion that the deck is mixed.

Square the pack and ask someone to cut the cards. Again the illusion is strengthened by the contrast between the top cards of the two halves.

Turn the deck over and square it. Pause to explain that you will now cause the cards to rearrange themselves so that they will all again be facing the same way. Do not mention the three selected cards.

Spread the deck on the table. Do not make a wide spread, and do not press on the cards as you spread them. Because face-to-face cards tend to stick together, it is likely that the three reversed cards will not show up in the spread! If this occurs, pause and say that you will now attempt to locate the three selected cards. Have these three cards named. Square the deck and spread again, this time applying pressure and making a wide spread. The sudden appearance of the face-up cards is very startling and provides a fitting climax to the trick.

If only one or two of the cards show up, remove them, and spread again. I have frequently had it happen that the first spread revealed no cards, and then three more spreads were necessary, one for each of the three selected cards! If this occurs, it is good showmanship to make the last spread with the cards face up. Remove the face-down card, have it named, and turn it over slowly for effect.

Smooth out your presentation, devise some appropriate patter, and you will have one of the flashiest and most novel effects in impromptu card magic.

FACE-TO-FACE FANTASY

The basic move of this effect, which enables you to place the two halves of a deck face to face, then suddenly find the cards all facing the same way again, is not original with me. It was invented by Japanese magician Tenkai, and shown to me by a Chicago magician who had reinvented it. It is certainly one of the most deceptive moves in card magic, and one that is surprisingly little used. My contribution to its use is to combine it in a somewhat novel manner with the discovery of two selected cards.

The effect of the trick is as follows. Two cards are selected by two members of the audience. They are returned to the deck, which is shuffled. The deck is divided in half. The lower half is turned over and the two halves are placed together again, face to face. The magician taps the cards and fans them. The cards are all seen to be backs upward again, with the exception of one card, which is face up in the center of the fan! This card is identified as one of the selected cards. Again the deck is divided and the two halves placed face to face. Another tap, and the deck is again fanned to reveal the cards all facing the same way, with the second selected card reversed in the center!

Method

White-border cards should be used. The two selected cards first are brought to the bottom of the deck. The Reversed Hindu Shuffle (described in the previous effect) is a convenient method of doing this.

It is now necessary for you to reverse, secretly, the two selected cards, so that they will be face up on the bottom of the pack. After a great deal of experimentation with different methods of doing this, I have become convinced that the following procedure is the simplest and least detectable.

Give the cards a riffle shuffle, holding the bottom card. Then spread the cards in your hands and call attention to the fact that the cards are all facing in the same direction. As you square the cards, obtain a break above the two selected cards, at the end of the deck nearest you. The break is held by the right thumb, with the right hand holding the deck as indicated in the picture below.

Probably the best way to get this break is to secure it first with the little finger of the left hand, then, as the right hand squares the cards and takes them from the left, transfer the break from the left little finger to the right thumb.

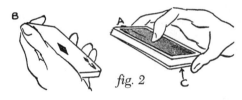

fig. 1

You now proceed to explain to your audience exactly what you intend to do next. Tell them that you intend to divide the deck in half. As you say this, the left hand approaches the right and cuts off half the deck. The left hand turns this half face up and permits it to rest on the palm.

If the above instructions have been followed correctly you will now have half the deck (face up) in the left hand and half the deck (face down) in the right hand. The left hand is holding the cards on its palm. The thumb is along the left side, as shown in the drawing below. The right hand is holding its half from above, between the thumb and middle finger. The deck is held by the ends as shown: with the thumb at the end nearer you and the middle finger at the opposite end. The thumb continues to hold the break at the lower right corner of the cards.

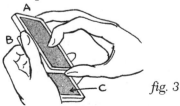

fig. 2

Explain to the audience that you intend to reverse half the cards (you have just done so with the left hand), and place the two halves face to face. Suiting action to words, the right hand places its half on top of the half in the left hand, but only for a brief instant. As soon as the halves are together the right thumb releases its hold on the two selected cards, and immediately the upper half is shoved forward so that it projects about an inch and a half beyond the lower portion.

fig. 3

The two cards are left on top of the lower half, but this fact is concealed because, while the move is being made, the left hand rotates to the right, exposing the undersides of the two halves. The right hand leaves the cards entirely, permitting the left hand to hold the two halves. The back of the left hand is uppermost. Point to the two halves of the deck, and call attention to the fact that they are now facing each other.

Take the cards in the right hand for a moment, then place them on the left palm. The picture below shows how they are held.

fig. 4

The left hand can now turn the cards over for a moment to show the back side, since the left palm hides the lower end of the upper half.

Explain that after placing the halves face to face, you intend to square the cards (make motions of squaring them with the right hand, but without touching the cards), then tap them on the corner (do so with the right hand), which will cause the lower half to magically reverse itself. As you say this, the right hand lifts up the upper half, holding it by the ends, between thumb and middle finger, thumb on end nearest you. The left hand turns the lower half over (so that it faces downward) and places it back on top of the upper half. The cards are now squared and held on the left palm, backs up. After this magic reversal has occurred, you continue to explain, the cards will again be facing the same direction. As you say this, fan through the cards, taking care not to expose the two reversed cards on the bottom of the fan. But, you add, one of the selected cards will be found reversed in the center of the fan.

Square the deck again and hold it on the left palm. You have now explained exactly the sort of trick you intend to perform, and in so doing you secretly have managed to reverse the two selected cards! They are now on the bottom of the deck.

Proceed to do what you have said you intended to do. The deck is in the left hand. The right hand begins to cut off about half the cards, holding them by the ends as shown.

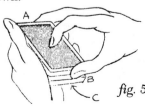

fig. 5

At this point a very curious move occurs, both hands acting simultaneously. As the right hand turns its half face up, the left hand turns over and places its half face down (apparently, but not actually) on top of the half in the right hand. The right half, however, is left projecting about an inch and a half upward. The illustration below shows this position.

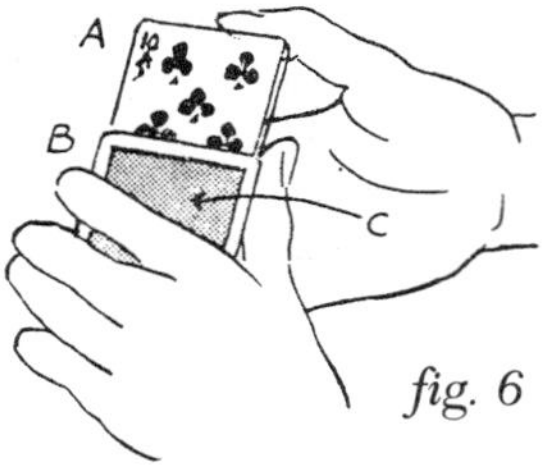

fig. 6

The best way to master this move is to hold the cards in the manner shown in figure 5. Then lift off the upper half and place the cards in the position shown in figure 6. Both hands reverse their halves simultaneously, then the left hand slaps its half against the half held in the right hand. It appears exactly as if you placed the two halves face to face. Actually, the deck is just as it was before, except that it has been turned over, and half the cards are projecting forward.

Take the cards in the right hand and place them on the left palm, as you did before when you explained what you intended to do. (See figure 4.) Turn the left hand over to give them a brief glimpse of the other side, then back again. Square the cards. To prove that the halves are actually face to face, slide off the upper card (which is the second selected card) and shove it into the center of the deck, face down. Then turn the deck over and do the same thing with the top card on the other side, shoving it in face down also.

Tap the deck (in the manner you tapped it previously) and command the lower half to reverse itself. Ask the second person who selected a card to name his card. Tap the deck again and command that card to turn over. Immediately fan through the deck to reveal the fact that all the cards are backs uppermost, with the exception of the selected card, which will be face up in the center! Take care, of course, not to expose the bottom card of the fan, which is still reversed. Remove the chosen card and place it on the table.

To find the other selected card, you go through almost the same procedure. The cards are placed on the left palm, the move is made, and the halves apparently are placed face to face. The left hand holds the cards, showing the backs momentarily, then the cards are squared and held in the left hand. The deck is now turned over, given one straight cut, and squared again. The cut will place the remaining selected card in the center, reversed!

Tap the cards once to straighten out the deck, then again to reverse the remaining selected card. Have it named, and immediately spread the cards face uppermost on the table. Slide out the face-down card in the center, and turn it over dramatically to conclude the effect.

DOUBLE-CLIMAX SPELLER

Nothing is essentially new in this effect, but the combination of principles is, I believe, unique. I have been using it for many years, and I know of no impromptu spelling effect that achieves such a spectacular effect at the expense of so little manipulation.

The effect is as follows. A card is selected and replaced. The deck is shuffled. The performer runs through about half the deck, asking the spectator to watch for his card. The spectator fails to see it. The magician believes, however, that he can find the card in a rather novel manner, by spelling to it: dealing a card from the top for each letter in the name of the card. He proceeds to do this. The spelling terminates correctly upon the card spelled by the magician, but this is not the card selected by the spectator. The magician looks puzzled, then remembers that the trick only works when the person who took the card does the spelling himself. He hands the deck to the spectator, who proceeds to spell the name of his card. The spelling terminates correctly upon the chosen card, which is face up in the deck! It can readily be seen why I have called this effect the Double-Climax Speller. The fact that the magician spells correctly to a card, even though it is the wrong one, is a trick in itself. That the spectator can then spell to the correct card is a sufficient climax, and when the card pops at him, face up, this second climax tops even the first. It never fails to produce an enthusiastic response.

Method

The means of working this effect are absurdly simple. The selected card is first brought to the second-from-the-top position. I prefer to use the Erdnase in-jog shuffle (described on page 1).

After the shuffle, hold the cards in the left hand, and secure a break beneath the second card from the top with the tip of the left little finger, as if you were about to make a double lift. Instead of making the lift, however, you turn the top card face up on top of the deck. Square the cards (continuing to hold the break as shown in figure 1, on the next page) and ask if the shuffle by any chance brought the selected card to the top.

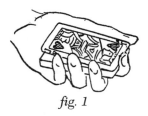

fig. 1

When the spectator says "No," make a double lift, holding the cards at the lower right corner, between your right thumb and fingers. Move the card a few inches to the right. The left hand now turns the pack over and places it on top of the two cards. In appearance, you have shown the top card, then replaced it on top of the deck. Actually, the selected card is now reversed on the top of the pack! Your patter excuse for turning the deck over is to ask if the shuffle accidentally brought the card to the bottom. Again the spectator says "No." Square the cards by tapping them on the table, which gives you an easy opportunity to glimpse the reversed card!

Hold the cards face up in the left palm and begin to run through them, asking the spectator to tell you if the selected card appears. As you run through the cards, spell the name of the selected card silently to yourself, running one card for each letter. As soon as you have completed this silent spelling, notice the *next* card. Continue to run the cards, spelling silently the name of this card. Be careful not to give away this break in your mental spelling by hesitating as you run the cards from left to right. Run them slowly and smoothly. Begin your spelling on the card itself. When this second spelling terminates, pause and ask the spectator if the selected card has been seen. As you ask this, separate the cards at the point where the spelling ended. Your right hand will now hold about half the deck. When the spectator says "No," replace the cards in your right hand *beneath* the cards in your left, square the pack, turn it face down, and hold it in the left hand.

State that you will attempt to locate the card by spelling it. Start spelling the name of the wrong card, turning each card over and placing it face up on the table. Your spelling ends on the card, but it is not the chosen one. Hand the deck to the spectator and ask him to spell his card. When his spelling terminates, his selected card will be face up on the top of the deck!

After you become familiar with the routine you can make it still more effective by adding a third card! While you are running through the deck, asking the spectator to watch for the selected card, do not cut the cards at the point suggested above, but notice the *next* card again and continue running cards until you have spelled it also. You can forget the name of the chosen card. You merely have to remember the two cards that are *not* the chosen one. After you have spelled the wrong card, try a second time to locate the card by spelling. This second attempt (though it terminates on the card spelled) fails also. Then hand the deck to the spectator for the climax! If you emphasize the fact that the deck is shuffled before the trick is started, your audience will give you credit for some rapid and ingenious card stacking!

NEVER-MISS STOP EFFECT

Stop tricks come and go. Maybe you can use this one. It requires a setup, but has the merit of being surefire. The setup is never suspected.

Twenty cards are dealt from the top of the deck and placed aside. A card is selected from the remainder of the deck, it is replaced, and the cards are shuffled and placed on the table. The twenty cards are spread face up for a moment while the magician calls attention to the fact that they represent values all the way from one to thirteen. The twenty cards are squared and held face down in the left hand. The right hand deals them to the table, face up, one at a time. The spectator is asked to call "Stop" at any point. The numerical value of the card selected in this manner is noted. The rest of the deck, which contains the chosen card, is handed to the spectator, who counts from the top of the deck and finds the chosen card at the number indicated.

Method

The setup involves fifteen cards. Remove the tens and the jacks from the deck. Mix these eight cards together so that they are not arranged in any order. Then remove seven indifferent cards from the deck and place them with the jacks and tens so that there is an indifferent card between every pair of jacks or tens. In other words, every other card is either a jack or ten. There will be fifteen cards in all. The first and last cards will be either jacks or tens. These fifteen cards are placed on top of the pack.

Begin the trick by giving the deck an overhand shuffle, holding the top-stock (the Erdnase in-jog shuffle, described on page 1), then deal twenty cards to the table. Push this pile aside. Fan the rest of the pack for the selection of a card. As you fan the cards, count ten cards down from the top and attempt to force the eleventh card. If you force it, emphasize the fact that you are having the card replaced at the same spot from which it was taken. If you fail to force the card, hold a break under the tenth card, so that when the card is replaced it becomes the eleventh card. After the card is returned, give the deck a quick overhand shuffle, holding the top-stock, and set the pack aside.

Pick up the twenty cards and spread them face up, calling attention to the fact that many different values are represented. Square the cards and begin dealing them slowly, placing them face up on the table. The first five cards are indifferent cards. As you deal these five, ask the spectator to tell you to stop at any card he desires. By the time you finish saying this, the five cards will have gone by. When he calls "Stop," it is a simple matter for you to make it appear as if he stopped on a ten or jack. If you have a ten or jack in your hand, simply place it aside, stating its value. If you do not, merely continue dealing that card and turn over the next card, that is, the top card of the pile in your left hand. After you show the card (either ten or jack), show the two cards that were on either side of it and call attention to the fact that, had he stopped you a moment earlier or a moment later, he would have selected a card of totally different value.

Pick up the rest of the pack and hand it to the spectator with the request that he count down to the number indicated. If the number was ten, ask him to count ten cards and then turn up the next one. If he stopped on a jack, ask him to look at the eleventh card!

Another effective method of handling the "Stop" part of the trick is to spread the cards face up, then move your finger slowly from one end of the spread to the other, asking him to stop you at any point he wishes. Have your finger some distance above the spread, so that spectators will be unsure at which card it is pointing, when you are told to stop.

The tens and jacks are so different in appearance that there is little likelihood that any setup will be detected.

BIG CASINO COUNTDOWN

Nine cards are selected from a deck. The names are jotted down on a piece of paper. The nine cards are spread, face up, on the table, and the spectator is asked to mentally select any card. The cards are then placed in the center of the deck. The performer chooses a card at random from the deck, then takes the deck and this card behind his back, stating that he will insert the card face up into the pack. He does so. The deck is spread, backs upward, on the table to reveal the reversed card somewhere near the center. The performer states that if the trick is successful, this reversed card will enable him to locate the card that the spectator selected mentally. He proceeds to do this.

Method

I have called this effect the Big Casino Countdown because it employs the ten of diamonds (the "Big Casino" card)—a card that may easily be remembered. Before beginning the effect, the ten is reversed and placed in the position of ninth card from the *bottom* of the deck.

Fan the upper portion of the deck and have nine cards removed. Mix these nine cards together, then spread them in a fan on the table. Ask someone to select a card mentally. To make certain that this card will not be incorrectly remembered, jot down the names of the nine cards on a piece of paper. Then square the fan and place it on top of the deck. Give the deck one cut to bury the cards in the center.

Remove any card from somewhere near the top of deck, but do not show its face. Place the deck and this card behind your back, stating that you will insert this card face up into the center of the deck. Actually, you merely place the card on top, then bring the deck back to the front. Spread it on the table to reveal the ten of diamonds reversed near the center. State that you will use this card to locate the one that has been selected by the spectator.

Ask for the name of the chosen card, and check it with the list. Its position on the list determines the manner in which you employ the ten of diamonds for a countdown. A reference to the following table will make clear the modus operandi. The numbers indicate the position of the card on the list.

1. Divide the spread just above the ten, squaring the lower half. Turn the ten face down on top of this packet. Then count to the tenth card.
2. Divide the spread *below* the ten, and count to the tenth card.
3. Divide below the ten, count ten cards, then turn over the *next* card.
4. Divide above the ten, turn the ten face down on top of the lower half, and spell "ten of diamonds," ending on the selected card.
5. Divide below the ten, and spell "ten of diamonds."
6. Divide below the ten, spell "ten of diamonds," and turn the *next* card.
7. Divide above the ten, turn the ten face down on top of the lower half, and spell "the ten of diamonds," ending on the correct card.
8. Divide below the ten, and spell "the ten of diamonds."
9. Divide below the ten, spell "the ten of diamonds," and turn the *next* card.

In short, the ten of diamonds can be used in a perfectly natural manner for a countdown that ends upon the card the spectator mentally selected!

The list is very easy to memorize if you note the following points. The nine positions on the list can be broken into three groups, with three in each group. If the card is in the first group of three, you use only the value of the card—that is, you count ten cards to the selected one. If the card falls in the second group of three, then you spell "ten of diamonds." If it falls in the last group, you add "the" to the name of the card. After you note to which group of three the card belongs, then note whether it is the first, second, or third card in that group. If it is the first card, you break above the ten, and turn the ten back over to use it in the counting or spelling. If the second card in the group, you break below the ten and end your count (or spelling) on the selected card. If the third card, you follow the same procedure, but turn the *next* card after counting (or spelling) has terminated.

There are four other cards in the deck that may be used in the same manner as the ten of diamonds. They are the nine of spades, nine of hearts, jack of diamonds, and queen of diamonds. To determine in what position to place them at the beginning of the trick, subtract one from their value. Thus, if you use the queen of diamonds, it must be placed (reversed) at the eleventh position from the bottom of the deck.

The trick will not bear repetition, but if you remember the five cards that can be used, you may find it easier to make the setup, using whichever card you locate first.

SIX-OF-SPADES COUNTDOWN

The effect of this trick is similar to that of the previous one, except that seventeen (rather than nine) cards may be used. It is a little more difficult to perform, since it requires more memory work. I believe the effect is well worth the extra effort, though.

Method

Before the trick is started, the six of spades is placed second from the top of the deck. Shuffle the cards without disturbing the position of the six, then deal seventeen cards from the top of the deck to form a row of face-up cards on the table. Someone is asked to make a mental selection of a card.

As in the previous trick, the cards are jotted down on paper for future reference. Replace the cards on top of the deck. Be sure to replace them in the correct order, so that the order of cards from top to bottom in the deck will correspond to the order from top to bottom on your list.

Fan the deck to show that the cards are all facing the same direction.

Give the deck a cut, but hold the break with the tip of the left little finger (if the cards are held in the left hand). Immediately place the deck behind your back, stating that you will reverse a single card somewhere near the center. The card you reverse is the six of spades, which is the second card beneath the break. Bring the deck to the front again and place it (back up) on the table.

Ask for the name of the selected card. If it happened to be the six of spades, then you are ready to perform a miracle. Merely spread the cards and call attention to the fact that only the six is reversed in the deck! If the selected card is not the six, state that you have reversed a card that will enable you to locate the card that has been selected.

Spread the deck to reveal the six of spades. It is then used, in the following manner, to reveal the chosen card. The numbers refer, as before, to the position of the card on your list.

1. Turn over the card just *above* the reversed six.
2. (This is the six of spades.)
3. Turn the card just *below* the six.
4. Break the spread *above* the six, turn the six over on top of the lower half of the spread, and spell "six," terminating on the card.
5. Break the spread *below* the six, spell "six."
6. Same as above, but turn the *next* card.
7. Break above the six, turn the six over, count down six cards.
8. Break below the six, count six cards.
9. Break below the six, count six, turn next card.
10. Break above the six, turn the six over, spell "six spades," terminating on the chosen card.
11. Break below the six, spell "six spades."
12. Break above the six, turn the six over, spell "six of spades."
13. Break below the six, spell "six of spades."
14. Break below the six, spell "six of spades," and turn the next card.
15. Break above the six, turn the six over, spell "the six of spades."
16. Break below the six, spell "the six of spades."
17. Break below the six, spell "the six of spades," and turn the next card.

The list is not so difficult to memorize as it might seem. It can be broken into the following sections:

1. card above	4. ⎫	7. ⎫
2. six of spades	5. ⎬ spell "six"	8. ⎬ count six cards
3. card below	6. ⎭	9. ⎭
10. ⎫ spell	12. ⎫ spell	15. ⎫ spell
11. ⎭ "six spades"	13. ⎬ "six of spades"	16. ⎬ "the six of spades"
	14. ⎭	17. ⎭

After the card is named, check it on the list. When you do this, note into which group it falls, using the above as a mental key. This will tell you what to spell or count. Then its position in the group will tell you where to make the break and how to do the spelling or counting. The rules for this are the same as in the previous effect.

The six of hearts may be substituted for the six of spades, as their names include the same number of letters. I am not aware of any other card that can be used in this manner to cover as many as seventeen cards.

TWO PILES AND SUBTRACT

This trick is similar in its effect to a trick once shown to me by Paul Rosini. The method of working, however, is quite different from the method employed by Mr. Rosini.

About twenty cards are dealt to the table to form a row. A card is mentally selected. The row is replaced on the deck; then the deck is shuffled and is cut to form two piles. A pile is selected by a spectator, and the selected card is discovered in a novel manner.

Method

Before the trick is shown, the cards in the fifth and seventh positions from the top must be sixes. The suit of the sixes does not matter.

Deal the cards to the table to form a vertical row of overlapping cards. It makes no difference how many cards are in the row, provided you do not exceed twenty-six. About twenty cards is a convenient number.

Have the card mentally selected, and ask a spectator to count to the card from the top of the row. The spectator must remember both the card and the number that represents its position from the top. Replace the row on top of the deck without changing the order of the cards.

The deck is now given a false overhand shuffle. In describing the shuffle I will assume that the reader is familiar with the Erdnase in-jog for holding the top-stock (described on page 1).

The deck is held in the left hand. The right hand undercuts about half the deck. Before the false shuffle begins, the left thumb in-jogs the top card of the half it holds. Shuffle the cards from the right hand on top of this jogged card. Then cut to the jogged card (leaving it on the bottom). Run four cards, one at a time, then in-jog the fifth card, and throw the rest on top. This completes the shuffle. Square the pack (keeping the in-jog) and ask the spectator to tell you the number of the selected card, that is, how far it was down from the top of the row.

If the number is one, five, six, or seven you can produce the card immediately.

If number one: turn over the deck to reveal the chosen card on the bottom.

If number five: cut the deck *below* the in-jog, and turn up the top card of the lower half.

If number six: cut below the in-jog as before, and show the bottom card of the upper half (the in-jogged card). Or, if you prefer, state that somehow the shuffle has left one card projecting slightly from the center. Turn the deck around and let the spectator pull out the in-jogged card, which will be the chosen one.

If number seven: turn over the top card of the deck.

In most cases the spectator will choose the fifth, sixth, or seventh card. Sometimes, just to fool you, someone will select the first card. That is why the trick is designed to take care of the first, fifth, sixth and seventh cards in some special manner.

If the number is other than one, five, six, or seven you proceed in a different way. Cut the deck *below* the in-jog, to form two piles on the table. The illustration below shows the position of the first, fifth, sixth, and seventh cards after the piles have been formed. Pile A has been cut from the top of Pile B and placed to the right. The fifth and seventh cards will be the top cards of the two piles. In other words, the top card of each pile will be a six.

Tell the spectator that the trick will involve a slight bit of subtraction. Have the spectator turn over the top card of either pile. It makes no difference which is chosen, since in either case it will be a six.

If the number of the chosen card is above six, then six must be subtracted from that number. The remainder will indicate the position of the chosen card in pile A! Let us suppose that the number was seventeen. Six from seventeen is eleven. The spectator is asked to count down to the eleventh card in pile A. It will be the selected card. Make it appear as if the spectator selected the right-hand pile by the following ruse. If the six was turned over on top of pile A, turn the six face down again and shove that pile forward toward the spectator, saying to count to the eleventh card. If, on the other hand, the six was turned over on the left-hand pile, pile B, leave the six face up and say to count to the eleventh card in the *other* pile!

If the number of the chosen card is below six, then subtract the number from six. The remainder indicates the position of the card in the *left*-hand pile! Suppose the number was four. Four from six is two. The card is second from the top in the left-hand pile. This pile is forced upon the spectator in the manner explained above.

Don't ask me how such a short shuffle can produce such a complicated setup, but it does. If correctly executed, the trick never fails to work.

Eugene Bernstein has developed an interesting variation of this trick. No setup is required. Gene merely glances at the first, fifth, sixth, and seventh cards, then devises a method of adding or subtracting them so that he can secure a six. This nearly always can be done. If one of the cards is a six, then there is nothing more to worry about. If there is a five and an ace, then the two added together make six. Or maybe a four can be subtracted from a ten to leave six—a six must somehow be secured from the four cards. Then, after the two piles are made, later in the trick, Gene simply shows the desired cards, combines them to produce a six, and goes on with the trick from there. By using a little ingenuity, and forcing the right packets, he can make the trick seem like a miracle!

EYE-POP ROUTINE

Magicians will hardly be fooled by this short and snappy piece of card conjuring, but most audiences will find it something of a real eyepopper. Give it a try and see for yourself.

Method

Before beginning the trick, secure four cards: the seven of clubs, seven of spades, eight of clubs, and eight of spades. Place the seven of spades and eight of clubs on top. The seven of clubs and eight of spades are placed on the bottom of the deck, reversed.

Riffle-shuffle the deck, holding your top- and bottom-stock. Give the deck an apparent cut by pulling out the center portion and slapping it on top, but hold a break above the seven of spades and eight of clubs. Force these two cards on a spectator. Ask the person to remember them. Then place them on the top of the pack.

Give the deck a single cut and square it. Snap the end of the deck with your fingers, stating that you will cause the two cards to reverse themselves. Fan the deck to reveal the seven of clubs and the eight of spades.

The spectator naturally will think these are the same two cards. Before anyone has a chance to look too closely, however, you make the following move. Hold the fanned deck in your right hand. The left hand takes the portion of fan to the left of the reversed cards, squares it, turns it face up, and replaces it *behind* the two cards. The left hand now takes the cards, while the right hand removes the portion of fan to the right of the two cards, turns it over also, and replaces it on top of the two cards.

This move has the double merit of (1) placing the two selected cards in the center of the deck, facing the same way as the other cards and (2) bringing the two originally selected cards to the top of the deck.

Square the pack, stating that you will now cause the two cards to jump from the center of the deck to the top. Snap the deck, then turn over the two top cards to prove it. Thus, you conclude the trick with the same two cards the spectator had previously taken.

If you run through the trick rapidly, there is little likelihood that the spectator will notice that the two reversed cards were not the same as the ones originally selected. Other cards than the ones suggested here can, of course, be employed.

SYMPATHETIC DECKS

Two decks are employed in this effect. Both may be thoroughly shuffled by the spectator before the trick begins. For convenience in description, we will assume that one deck has blue backs and the other red backs.

The performer states that the trick involves the use of two cards that are alike in both value and color, such as the two red aces. The spectator is given a free choice of what these two cards will be. Let us assume that the two red aces are chosen.

The blue deck is picked up and the two red aces are removed. The performer fans the deck, requesting the spectator to touch a card somewhere near the center. After this is done, the two red aces are placed in the deck, reversed, on either side of the chosen card. The deck is squared and placed aside. No one, not even the spectator, has seen the face of the chosen card, but the two red aces mark its position in the deck.

The red deck is now picked up. The red aces are removed and placed in the center of the deck, reversed, one on top of the other.

The magician patters about the state of sympathy that exists between the two packs of cards. The red deck, he says, will attempt to imitate the state of affairs that exists in the blue deck. To prove it, he fans the blue deck, and the chosen card is removed and turned over. Let us assume it is the jack of clubs. The red deck is likewise fanned, and to everyone's astonishment, there is now a face-down card between the two reversed aces! The card is withdrawn and turned over. It also is the jack of clubs!

Method

When the reversed aces (or whatever cards are selected by the spectator) are placed on either side of the chosen card, they are left projecting about halfway from the end of the deck. The deck is squared.

It is now necessary to obtain secretly a glimpse of the chosen card. After considerable experimentation I have devised two methods of getting this glimpse. They seem to be of about equal merit. You can adopt the one that suits you better.

Glimpse number one: Hold the deck in the left hand, facing toward you as shown in the picture below. As the right fingers push the aces into the deck, the chosen card will be pushed out at the other end.

fig. 1

This is hidden from the audience by the left palm. Allow the chosen card to be pushed out just far enough to reveal its index, then shove it into the deck with the right thumb, and square the deck. With a little practice this move can be made smoothly and rapidly.

Glimpse number two: Hold the deck upright in the left hand as shown below, back to the audience. Call attention to the names of the two aces. As you name the ace in front, point to it with the fingers of the right hand. When you name the ace in the rear, the right fingers bend this card back in order to show it to the audience. (See the illustration below.)

fig. 2

If the deck is held loosely by the left hand, the bending of the ace will cause the deck to break slightly, above the chosen card. This permits a quick glimpse of the index as shown in the picture.

After you have obtained the name of the chosen card (by either of the above methods), square the deck and place it aside, with the back of the deck uppermost.

Pick up the red deck and fan it with the faces toward yourself. Hold the cards so that the faces are visible only to you. Pretend to be hunting for the red aces. As soon as you find one, do not indicate the fact, but state that the red aces seem to be difficult to locate. As you say this, give the deck a cut, bringing the red ace to the top, then pretend to begin looking again. This time, you look for the chosen card. When you find it, very openly take it and place it on top of the deck. State that you finally found one of the aces. Now look for the second ace. When you find it, place it on top. As you do this, casually lower the fan so that the audience can actually see you remove this ace and place it on top.

At this point you have the two aces on top of the deck, with the chosen card between them. The audience thinks, however, that both aces are on top. Turn the deck backs up, and as you square it, obtain a break beneath the chosen card, holding it with the tip of the little finger.

Turn over the top ace, naming it, and square it with the card beneath. The right hand then makes a double lift, holding the cards by the ends, thumb on lower end, middle finger at other end. The lower left corner of the ace (really two cards) is now used to flip over the other ace, which is on top of the deck. Name it as you do so.

One ace is now face up on top of the deck. The right hand apparently holds the other ace, also face up. Drop the cards from the right hand on top of the ace on the deck, then square the pack and make a single cut. To the audience, the moves have been perfectly natural. Apparently you have reversed the two aces and placed them together in the center of the deck.

The rest of the trick should now be clear.

It might be of interest to mention that the move described above can also be used for a novel discovery of a chosen card. The card is brought to second from top. The two top cards apparently are reversed (in the same manner that the aces were reversed) and the deck is cut. The card is named, the deck is fanned, and the card is found face down between the two reversed cards.

VANISHING AND REAPPEARING CARD

A selected card is caused to vanish from the deck, then reappear in a re-markable manner.

Method

Before the trick is started, the bottom card of the deck must be reversed.

Riffle-shuffle the pack, holding the bottom card. Because it is reversed, be careful not to let the audience catch a glimpse of it. Square the deck and hold it in your left hand. With the right hand, riffle the front end of the deck. Invite a spectator to insert a finger into the cards at any chosen point.

Divide the deck at that point. Turn over the top half and call the spectator's attention to the bottom card of that half. Let us assume that it is the ace of clubs. The two halves of the deck are now placed together, face to face. The half that has the ace showing goes beneath the other half.

Square the deck, then turn it over *three* times. After this has been done, state that the ace of clubs has vanished. To prove it, fan the deck, and call attention to the fact that the face-up card, at the point where the two halves meet face to face, is not the ace of clubs. The audience naturally supposes that the *face-down* card at the point of contact—that is, the bottom card of the upper half—is the ace. Square the upper half, turn it over, and place it face up on top of the other cards. To everyone's surprise, the bottom card of this half is not the ace either!

As you square the cards (the deck is face up in the left hand), secure a break under the second card (which is the ace of clubs), holding it with the tip of the little finger in preparation for a double lift. The cards are now passed one at a time from the left hand to the right, as if the right hand were counting them. The spectator is asked to watch for the ace of clubs. The first card taken by the right hand is, of course, the double card. I have found that the easiest way of doing this is first to slide the card about an inch to the right. Then the left thumb holds the card on the deck, while the right hand changes its position so that it can begin taking the cards as if you were counting them.

After the entire deck has been run through, state that the ace seems to have vanished. Square the pack and hold it face down in your left hand. (The ace is now the top card.)

At this point you offer to explain to the audience just how the ace vanished. First, you say, the deck was riffled and someone inserted a finger. As you say this, riffle the end and have the spectator insert a finger once more. Following exactly the same moves as before, you then reverse the upper half of the deck (calling attention to the fact that the bottom card of this half had previously been the ace of clubs) and place the two halves face to face. Before placing the halves together, however, show the face-up cards of each half, so that the audience will see that neither is the ace of clubs.

At this point an important move occurs. The left hand is holding one half of the deck, face up (the top card of this half is the ace). The right hand holds the other half, face down. Place the halves together, face to face, but let the upper half project about an inch over the right side of the lower half. (See figure 1.) As shown in the picture (figure 2), the left fingers slide the ace from the top of the half held in the left hand, so that the ace is flush with the half held in the right hand. This is kept concealed from the audience by tilting the cards forward. Figure 2 shows the move from the underside.

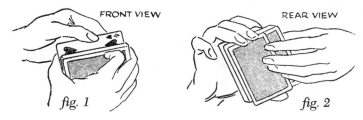

fig. 1   *fig. 2*

FRONT VIEW   REAR VIEW

As soon as the ace is flush with the half held in the right hand, the right hand withdraws its half, taking the ace with it, then immediately returns, and the two halves are placed face to face. The ace is now the lower card at the point of contact between the two halves.

Continue with your patter about how the ace originally vanished. Turn the deck three times, as before, and fan the cards, stating that when this had been done before, the ace had vanished. Add that the turning of the deck was confusing, and many thought that perhaps the ace was the lower card of the other portion of the deck, "but that was not the ace either." As you say this, reverse the upper half of the fan to reveal the ace of clubs! Look surprised and say, "Well, anyway, I'm glad we found the ace."

There is a simpler method of concluding this effect that eliminates the above sleight entirely. Perhaps it is just as effective.

After you have run through the cards to prove that the ace has vanished, square the deck and give it one overhand shuffle. The purpose of this shuffle is to transfer the ace from the top to the bottom of the deck. This is easily done by simply sliding the ace off the top first, then shuffling the other cards on top of it.

Square the cards and begin your patter about how the ace had vanished. Riffle the end and have the finger inserted. Reverse the upper half, and place the halves face to face without showing the ace as the bottom card of one of the halves. Before placing the halves together, however, point to the face-up card on the lower half to remind the audience that the ace had been in that position just before it had vanished. After the deck is squared, turn it three times, explaining that after you had done this before and fanned the deck, the ace had mysteriously disappeared. As you say this, fan the deck to reveal the ace at the point of contact between the halves!

IMPROVED LIE SPELLER

The original version of this effect of mine first appeared in Joe Berg's second book, *Here's More Magic.* Joe kindly gave me permission to present a more elaborate effect based upon the same principle.

A card is selected by each of two spectators and returned to the deck, which is shuffled. The performer states that he will locate the first selected card by spelling the answers to three different questions. He asks for the color of the card, its suit, and, lastly, whether the card was odd or even in value. A card is dealt to the table for each letter in the answers. The spelling terminates on the correct card.

The cards on the table are replaced on the deck, which is shuffled once more. Turning to the second spectator, the magician offers to find his card in a like manner, but with this additional feature. The spectator may lie if he wishes! That is, if his card was a red card he may say that it was a black card. He does not have to lie, but if he wishes he may give an incorrect answer to one or more of the three questions. Regardless of this, however, the spelling again terminates upon the chosen card!

Method

When you fan the deck to have the two cards selected, count the cards from the top of the fan and attempt to force the fourteenth and fifteenth cards. If the force fails it does not matter. Merely hold the break below the thirteenth card and have the two cards replaced so that they are in the fourteenth and fifteenth positions from the top of the deck. If the force is successful, then have the cards replaced at the spot from which they were taken.

Give the deck a false overhand shuffle, holding the top-stock. Turn first to the spectator whose card is fourteenth in the deck. The procedure that enables you to terminate the spelling on the fourteenth card is as follows.

Ask if the card is red or black. Spell the answer.

Ask for the suit. The suits are spelled as follows: hearts, spade, diamond, clubs. Note that the final *s* is omitted from the words "diamonds" and "spades." You can make this spelling seem more natural by asking your question in the form "Was the card a diamond or a heart?" If the spectator says diamond, then spell "diamond." If the person says heart, it will not seem unnatural to spell "hearts." If the card was black, of course, you ask, "Was it a spade or a club?"

Ask if the value of the card was odd or even. At this point you follow one of two alternative actions, depending on the suit of the card.

1. If the suit was spades, clubs, or diamonds: Spell o-d-d, and turn the *next* card. It will be the chosen one. Or spell e-v-e-n and turn the last card on the letter *n*.

2. If the suit was hearts: Get the tip of your little finger beneath the second card from the top, in preparation for a double lift. If the answer is odd, you will have to make the lift, dealing the first two cards as one, then continuing with single cards. After spelling o-d-d, turn the *next* card. If the answer is even, you can withdraw the little finger from the break. Simply spell e-v-e-n, and turn the *next* card.

It will be seen from a study of the above that the double lift will have to be made only if the card is an odd heart. Since only about one-eighth of the deck consists of odd hearts, the double lift will seldom be necessary.

The procedure is not difficult to memorize. After a few practice trials you will find it very easy to recall the manner in which the answers are to be handled.

After the first selected card has been found by spelling to it, toss the card aside and replace the pile on the table on top of the deck. The second selected card is now in the fourteenth position. Give the deck a false overhand shuffle as before.

Invite the spectator to attempt to thwart your success by giving incorrect answers. Naturally, it makes no difference what answers you get. By following the method just explained, you cause the spelling to terminate once more on the correct card.

If you want to perform the trick with only one spectator, have the person replace the chosen card in the fourteenth position. Then, after you have spelled to the card by using the correct answers, replace the card on top of the deck and put the thirteen cards on the table back on top. State that the trick would have worked just as well even if you had been lied to. To prove it, false-shuffle the deck, then repeat the spelling, utilizing the *incorrect* answers.

DO AS I DO

Ted Annemann graciously gave me permission to reprint an effect of mine that appeared in the Winter Extra, 1937–1938, issue of the *Jinx*.

Up to a certain point the procedure is similar to that of the familiar Do As I Do effect, involving two decks of cards. The performer and a spectator both shuffle a deck. Each selects a card, places it on top of the pack, and cuts the deck to bury the card in the center. The decks are exchanged. Each finds the chosen card in the pack now being held, then places his card face down on the table. So far the routine is familiar. In the usual version these two cards are turned over and shown to be alike. In my version a more startling climax is obtained.

The chosen cards are placed face down, just to the right of each deck. The performer states that the method of working the trick is very simple. To know the name of the spectator's card, it is only necessary to look at the top card of the other deck. As this is said, the top card of that deck is turned over, and so is the spectator's card. These two cards are identical! The performer goes on to say that the spectator can ascertain the name of the magician's card by following the same procedure. The top card of the spectator's deck is turned, and so is the magician's chosen card. They also are identical!

Method

While the decks are being shuffled, try to obtain a glimpse of the bottom card of the spectator's deck. If you fail to do this, remember the bottom card of your deck, then trade decks before you start the trick, making some remark to justify the exchange.

We will assume, then, that you know the bottom card of the deck held by the spectator. Each of you fans the deck, with the faces toward yourselves, and selects a card. The card is placed on top of the fan, and the deck is squared.

The card that you select in this manner must be the same as the card that is on the bottom of the spectator's deck.

Each deck is now given a single cut. The cut you make, however, is a false one. It is never detected because the spectator is too preoccupied with cutting the other deck.

I have found that the simplest and best of all false cuts to use in this connection is made as follows. The deck is held in the left hand, as shown in figure 1. The back of the deck is toward the audience. The deck must be held in a vertical position. This is very important. Many magicians are familiar with this cut but fail to secure the proper illusion because they tend to hold the deck parallel with the floor. The cards must be perpendicular to the floor as shown, and to the left side of the body.

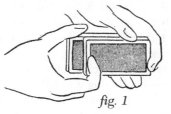

fig. 1

The right fingers seize the deck at the end nearer you (as shown above) and undercut the cards. This lower half is drawn back until it clears the remaining cards, then it is placed on the table with a slap. *The left hand does not move in any way.* The right hand now returns and takes the remaining half of the deck from the left, and slaps it on top of the cards on the table. All the work is done by the right hand. The left hand remains motionless throughout. The illusion is perfect. It looks, in fact, more convincing than a genuine cut made with the cards held in this same position!

After the decks have been apparently cut, they are traded. Again they are fanned, faces inward. The spectator is requested to look for the selected card in the deck now held, and to place it on top, while you do the same.

Look for the key card (the original bottom card, which you noted). It will be somewhere near the center. When you find it, square it with the card just *below* it, and remove these two cards as one, placing them on top of the fan.

The decks are squared and placed on the table. The top cards (that is, the chosen cards) are placed to the right of each deck. The rest of the trick is a matter of showmanship and patter. The top card of your deck matches the spectator's chosen card, and the top card of the spectator's deck matches your card.

I have let stand here the way I described this trick in *12 Tricks with a Borrowed Deck*. Friend Bert Allerton found a simple way to eliminate the false cut. When you fan the cards, break the fan above the key card. Your right hand, carrying its portion of the fan, moves forward to place the key card on the table. When your hand returns to the deck, it places its cards *behind* the cards in your left hand. In other words, in the act of placing the key card on the table, the deck unobtrusively is cut. Then the deck is squared and put down by the key card.

Incidentally, the false cut I described, shown to me by Joe Berg, also

can be improved. I mention it here even though Allerton's handling eliminates a false cut. Instead of holding the deck as pictured, its back toward
the audience, turn your left hand so that the deck, still perpendicular to
the floor, is pointed directly toward the audience. When you remove the
top half of the deck, your left hand keeps spectators from seeing which
half of the deck you withdrew.

As soon as the top half is taken, quickly rotate your left wrist and release the deck with your thumb, allowing it to fall flat on your palm. Your
right hand then slaps its half on top of the other half. I believe this to be
the simplest, easiest, and most effective of all false cuts.

A CLOSE FIT

Bert Allerton, that genial genius of the pasteboards whose subtle close-up
work won nationwide recognition, called my attention to this curious little optical illusion. Bert discovered it one day by accident and continued using it.

A small envelope, of the type that holds calling cards, is required. It
should be just large enough for a playing card to fit snugly inside. If you
use a bridge-size deck, the envelope should be a hair's breadth longer than
3½ inches and as much wider than 2¼ inches. It is a good plan to take a
card with you when you buy the envelope. I found mine at the dime store.

To present the illusion, spread the deck in a semicircle in front of you
on the table, with the faces of the cards showing. Place the envelope just
beneath the spread, as shown below. The envelope should be horizontal,
with the flap side up.

Offer to bet with anyone in the audience that you can place a playing
card inside this tiny envelope (emphasize that word "tiny") without bending or folding the card in any way. Everyone will swear that it can't be
done, and by gad, it does look impossible! For some strange optical reason the cards look much larger than the envelope!

To prove that it can be done, have someone select a card from the fan. Blow on it, then very slowly and openly slip it into the envelope and close the flap.

The trick lends itself to several patter angles. For example, you can act the part of a shoe salesman who convinces a customer that her foot is small enough to fit a certain shoe.

THE UNCONFUSED JOKER

If you have mastered the slip cut (a false cut that slips the top card to the center of the deck), you'll enjoy working this fast-moving little effect.

Take the joker (or any card you prefer) from the deck and place it aside. Tell the audience that you are going to use it in locating a selected card. Have a card selected and replaced on the top of the pack. Square the cards and place the joker face up on top of the chosen card.

At this point you apparently cut the deck. Actually you execute the slip cut. I find that the best way to make this cut is to keep the deck flat, a few inches above the table, with the hands holding it as shown in the illustration. The right hand quickly withdraws the upper half of the deck, with the exception of the top card (the reversed joker), which is held by the left forefinger. The right hand should withdraw the half by moving diagonally forward to the right. The left hand drops its half on the table and the right slaps its cards on top.

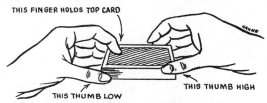

THIS FINGER HOLDS TOP CARD

THIS THUMB LOW

THIS THUMB HIGH

Practice making genuine cuts first, then repeat the same motions while retaining the top card with the finger. The cut should be made rapidly. The flat deck avoids bad angles if spectators are standing behind you. The fact that the top card is reversed makes the illusion of the cut perfect.

After the slip cut is made, spread the deck face down on the table and call attention to the fact that it will be a simple matter to locate the chosen card because you know that it is immediately beneath the reversed joker. (This is where the audience thinks it is, but actually it is still on top of the pack.)

However, you add, to make the trick more difficult, you are going to confuse the joker by placing it in a different part of the pack. Slide it from the fan and place it face up on top of the spread. Square the cards, give them a genuine cut, and spread them once more.

You continue by saying that the joker is a difficult card to confuse, and probably it has returned to the selected card already. Ask for the name of the card, then slide out the card beneath the joker and turn it over.

The use of a reversed top card to add to the illusion of the slip cut is, I believe, just beginning to be appreciated by card workers. There are many uses for it.

DOUBLE VANISH AND RECOVERY

Eddie Marlo, Chicago card wizard, figured this one out and gave me permission to include it here. The effect is beautiful and striking, and though practice is needed to execute it gracefully, no difficult moves are involved. Two selected cards are made to vanish by rubbing their faces together. Then each is located in a novel manner.

Begin the trick with two cards reversed on the bottom of the deck (unknown to the audience). Fan the deck for a fair selection of two cards. While the spectators are looking at their cards, secure a thumb break above the two bottom (reversed) cards, holding the pack in the right hand as shown in figure 1.

fig. 1

Ask for one of the selected cards, take it in the left hand, and place it on the bottom of the pack, squaring it with the two reversed cards so that the thumb now holds a slight break above the three cards.

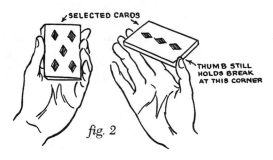

fig. 2

With the left hand, remove the top half of the deck and hold it face up as shown in figure 2. Extend the left hand and have the second selected card placed face up on top of the cards in that hand.

Turn the right hand over to show the bottom (selected) card. At this point the hands should be as in figure 2, each holding half the pack, with a chosen card facing the audience from each half.

RIGHT HAND MAKES CIRCULAR RUBBING MOTION

fig. 3

Announce that you are going to cause both cards to vanish. Bring the right hand over to the left (figure 3) and place the halves face to face. The back of the right hand is toward the audience.

Make a slight circular rubbing motion, and as you do so, transfer the three cards below the break from the right hand to the cards held in the left. Immediately separate the halves and allow each to lie flat on the palm of each hand, faces showing. Both selected cards have disappeared! With the thumb of each hand, slide the top cards to one side (figure 4) to expose the cards beneath. The cards beneath are also face up, and are not the selected cards! These moves should be practiced until they blend into a slow, graceful sequence. The vanish is very convincing.

BOTH CARDS SHOWN TO HAVE VANISHED

fig. 4

To recover the chosen cards, turn both halves face down and place the half in the right hand on top of the cards in the left. Give the deck a cut, then fan the cards to reveal one of the selected cards reversed in the center.

Break the fan just below the reversed card, so that the right hand holds the upper portion of the fan with the reversed card on the bottom. Extend the right hand toward the spectator who selected the card, asking him to take it for a moment. After he does so, replace the cards in the right hand below the cards held in the left. This puts the second selected card on the bottom of the deck.

Square the pack, then undercut three-fourths of the deck with the right hand and begin a Hindu Shuffle, pulling small packets of cards from the top of the half in the right hand and allowing them to fall on the cards in the left. Do this slowly.

Ask the spectator holding his card to place it face up on top of the cards in your left hand at any time he wishes. As soon as he does this, drop the cards remaining in the right hand on top of the cards in the left.

This places the second selected card face to face with the reversed one.

Snap the pack on the corner and command the two cards to come together. Fan the deck and remove the reversed card together with the card facing it. Turn the two cards over to reveal the face of the second selected card.

NAMING THE CARD CUT

So many of my magic friends have been caught off guard by this amusing trick that I feel justified in including it, though it is probably very old. Find an opportunity to reverse the bottom card of the deck secretly. Turn the deck over, keeping it well squared so that no one suspects that only the top card is face down, and place it on the table. Announce that if someone will lift up a portion of the cards, you will immediately name the card just below the cut.

Regardless of where the cut is made, of course, the card below it will be face up. Point to this card dramatically and say, "You cut to the eight of hearts"—or whatever the card happens to be.

Put the deck back into its proper shape before anyone picks it up to examine it. You will find that a lay audience will imagine that somehow the spectator cut to the only reversed card in the pack!

USE YOUR HEAD

In this effect you have to use your head. To be exact, you must use your forehead. Some years ago the forehead method of discovering a chosen card enjoyed a run of popularity. The card was brought to the top of the pack, and the pack was pressed against the forehead while the magician concentrated. The deck was then handed back to the spectator as if the trick had failed, leaving the selected card stuck to the performer's forehead. It was always good for a laugh.

Here's a new way of leading up to it. Before you begin the trick, locate the following thirteen cards and place them on the top of the deck, in any order—the four, five, nine, jack, and king of spades; the four, five, nine, jack, and king of hearts; and the seven, eight, and queen of clubs.

Count off these thirteen cards and hand them to a spectator with the request that he shuffle them. Turn your back and ask him to give the cards a cut, then note the card on the bottom of the packet. He is then to transfer cards from the top to the bottom, one at a time, spelling the name of the card he noted. While he is doing this and your back is turned, wet your finger and moisten the center of your forehead slightly.

Turn to the audience after the spelling is completed, and take the packet, placing it against your forehead so that the top card of the packet presses against the moist spot. This card will always be the selected one. Appear to concentrate a moment. Then hand back the cards, saying that you couldn't quite get the name of the chosen card, but that you would like to try the trick again. The card, of course, sticks to your forehead. Look surprised when you remove it.

THE SURPRISED GAMBLER

This is a rapid gambling expose with a surprise finish. Before the trick starts, have four aces on top of the deck. This is a good trick to use immediately following a four-ace effect, because all you have to do is leave the aces on top and false shuffle, and you're all set.

Tell the audience that the bottom deal is going out of fashion among gamblers because new and better methods have been devised. To prove it, you're going to demonstrate how gamblers once used the bottom deal, then how the modern method constitutes an improvement.

Go through the pack and remove the four kings. Show these cards and place them on the bottom of the deck. Give the deck a riffle shuffle, keeping the kings on the bottom and the aces on top. Follow with a false cut (the false cut described earlier in this book provides a nice flourish to use at this point). If you wish, you can show the audience that the four kings are still on the bottom of the deck.

Now deal five poker hands, one card at a time, but each time you deal to yourself make a very crude and open deal from the bottom, explaining as you do so that this is the way gamblers used to give themselves four of a kind. After the deal is completed, turn up your hand to show the four kings. Replace the other hands on top of the deck, then take the indifferent card from your hand and put it on top also. This leaves the four kings face up on the table.

Explain that in the new method of dealing, the four cards are not placed on the bottom but on the top of the deck. As you say this, place the four kings on top. Give the pack any kind of false shuffle that leaves the top half undisturbed. If you wish, you can pretend to be stacking the cards while you make this shuffle. Deal five more hands, asking the audience to watch the deal carefully to see if they can detect any fraud. All the cards are dealt fairly from the top.

After the deal, square up your five cards and turn the packet face up. This will reveal an indifferent card on the bottom. Look surprised, as if the deal had failed, then pretend to remember that your hand is supposed to have one indifferent card in it. "The four kings are beneath this card," you say, with complete confidence.

Slide the indifferent card away, revealing an ace. Look slightly embarrassed again. Then spread the four cards with your finger to reveal the four aces. "I seem to have lost the kings," you can say, "but at any rate I haven't lost the game!"

PAPER-CLIP DISCOVERY

There are lots of ways of using a paper clip to find a selected card, and maybe other card performers have worked out routines similar to this one. Bob Hummer and I combined ideas to produce it.

Before beginning, write on a small square of paper, "These are your selected cards." Clip it to the face of any card, using a large-size paper clip, and place this card on the bottom of the deck, the clip end toward you. To simplify the description, we will assume that this card is the ten of spades. The audience is not to know of the clip until the end of the effect.

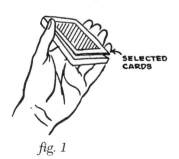

SELECTED
CARDS

fig. 1

Fan the pack and have two or three cards selected. Undercut the deck with the right hand, and do a Hindu Shuffle until someone says "Stop." Then have the selected cards placed on top of the cards in the left hand. Do not let the cards fall square with the others, however, but hold them in the fingers as shown in figure 1.

Now bring the half in the right hand (with the clip card on the bottom) over to the selected ones and slide it over them in such a way that the selected cards go between the piece of paper and the ten of spades. This is easy to do if you square the pack as soon as the selected cards have started to go under the clip, then force them flush with the deck. After this is done you should have the selected cards, the ten of spades, and the piece of paper all clipped together and in the center of the deck.

Your problem now is to get the ten of spades out of the clip. First give the deck an overhand shuffle, taking care not to expose the clip. Finish with the clipped cards still near the center.

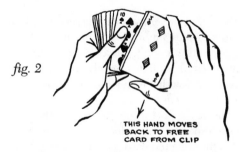

fig. 2

THIS HAND MOVES BACK TO FREE CARD FROM CLIP

Hold the deck in the left hand, with the clip toward you and the face of the pack showing. Ask if the exposed card on the bottom is one of the chosen ones. Of course, it isn't.

Now grasp the upper half of the pack with the right hand, and with the left thumb riffle the corners until you come to the ten of spades. Break the deck just above this card, and move the upper half to the right as shown in figure 2, exposing the upper left corner of the ten. Place your left thumb firmly on this corner and hold the card tightly as your right hand slides its half backward until it clears the deck. This pulls the ten from the clip (or, more accurately, pulls the clipped cards away from the ten) and leaves it face up on the cards in the left hand.

Point to the ten with the index finger of the right hand and ask if this is one of the selected cards. Again the answer is negative. If you wish, you can break the deck at some third point and ask the question a third time. Then shake your head as if the trick isn't working very well and hand the deck to someone, asking him to run through the cards to make sure the selected ones are still there.

What he finds, of course, will be the chosen cards neatly clipped together, with a note telling him that they were the ones selected.

VANISH AND SPELL

A selected card is made to vanish from the pack. It is found again by spelling to it from the top of the deck.

The selected card must first be brought to be second from the top. Use your favorite method. I prefer to glimpse the card after it is returned, then have the deck shuffled. Fan the cards with the faces toward you and pretend to find the card and slip it to the top of the deck. Actually, square the chosen card with the card above it in the fan and place these two cards, as one, on the top. Since you are going to show the top card anyway, this is a natural device for bringing the selected card to the second position.

We will assume, then, that the chosen card is second. Hold the cards in the left hand and spread them slightly with the thumb to permit the tip of your little finger to secure a slight break beneath the two top cards. Turn the top card face up and ask if it is the chosen one. It isn't, of course.

Square the reversed card with the selected card beneath it, and with the right hand lift off the two cards as one. The left hand immediately reverses the pack and places it on top of the two cards. Square the pack again and ask if the bottom card of the deck is the chosen one. This move automatically reverses the selected card, which is now on top of the deck.

Hold the deck in the left hand, face up, lift off about one-quarter of the pack, and spread it face up on the table. Ask the spectator if he sees his card there. When he says "No," turn the cards on the table face down. Then lift off another quarter of the deck, place it on top of the cards on the table, and spread it as you did with the previous portion. Again the chosen card is not found.

Once more turn the face-up cards over on the table so that all the cards on the table are face down. Again cut off a quarter of the pack, place it on top of the cards on the table, and spread it. After the spectator has failed to see his card, turn the face-up cards over as before to join the others.

When you repeat with the last quarter of the deck, the selected card (which is reversed) falls face down on top of the cards on the table. So when this last portion is spread, it likewise does not contain the chosen card!

The spectator has apparently seen every card, but the selected card has vanished!

As you spread out the last group of face-up cards, mentally run over them one at a time, spelling the name of the selected card. In many cases there will be just enough cards to make the spelling come out right. Remember that you can end the spelling on the card, or you can turn up the *next* one. If the cards are just the right number, all you have to do is turn them face down on top of the others, square the pack, and hand it out for spelling to the chosen card!

If there are too many cards in the group to make the spelling come out right, use this ruse. Pick up the face-down cards, leaving the face-up group on the table. After that, pick up the number of cards that you need for the spelling and place them on top of the others, leaving the few extra cards on the table as if by accident. Then casually pick up the extra ones and shove them into the center of the deck.

If the cards in the group are too few for the spelling, the best plan is to add the additional cards while giving the deck a false overhand shuffle, using an in-jog to hold the break.

DECK THROUGH HANDKERCHIEF

This is a slightly more elaborate version of a trick that I contributed some years ago to the *Jinx*.

In effect, two cards are selected and returned to the deck. The deck is wrapped in a handkerchief. The first selected card rises through the cloth. The magician then announces his intention of shaking the second card through the handkerchief, but to his apparent surprise the entire deck drops through! Then his face brightens when he discovers that a single card remains inside the handkerchief. It proves to be the second card selected.

THIS CORNER IS THROWN OVER DECK AND ARM

fig. 1

The two selected cards must be brought to the top of the deck. One of these cards is palmed off in the right hand, which goes under the handkerchief to hold the pack, as shown in figure 1. Note these points: (1) The card in the palm is *face up*, but the deck is placed face down on the hand, which is covered by the handkerchief; (2) The pack does not rest in the center of the cloth, but near the corner that falls over the right wrist.

Fold the corner by the wrist over the pack, then use the thumb and fingers of the left hand to grasp the end of the deck that is nearer the wrist. Raise the pack vertically as shown in figure 2. The thumb holds the card behind in place.

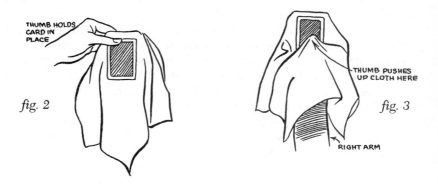

fig. 2

fig. 3

The right hand now goes under the handkerchief and grasps the lower part of the pack as in figure 3, with the fingers in front and the thumb pushing up the cloth in back as shown.

The left hand lets go of the deck and raises the front corner of the handkerchief to show the deck to the audience. This corner is thrown back so that it drops down behind, over the other corner, as in figure 4.

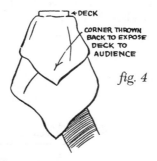

fig. 4

Turn the right hand over suddenly, throwing both of these corners forward over the deck, bringing the hand to the position shown in figure 5, seen from the side of the audience. The deck appears to be inside the handkerchief. Actually it is in back of the cloth, held in place by the fingers of the right hand!

fig. 5

BOTH CORNERS
HAVE BEEN
THROWN
FORWARD

fig. 6

FOREFINGER
IN BACK CAUSES
CARD TO RISE

The move is nothing more than an application to cards of the move used in the old trick of pulling a coin through a handkerchief. Wrap the cloth around the pack as in the standard effect of shaking a card through the cloth, and hold it in the right hand as shown in figure 6. The right forefinger in back now causes the top card of the deck (one of the selected ones) to rise upward.

Remove this card and state that you will attempt to shake the second card through the cloth.

Turn the right hand over as in figure 7 and hold the left hand beneath, as if to catch the card when it comes through. Give the handkerchief a shake, releasing your hold on the pack and allowing it to drop into the left hand, which immediately fans it.

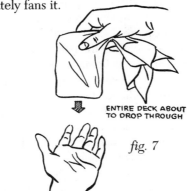

ENTIRE DECK ABOUT
TO DROP THROUGH

fig. 7

Appear to be surprised, then squeeze the cloth to show the outlines of a card inside. Snap it with your fingers, and take it out to have it identified as the second selected card.

THE SWIZZLE-STICK CIPHER

┌─────────────────────────────┐
│ ⅄onʁ ƨɘlɔɘ⊥ɘq   │
│ ɔɒʁq ʍiⅼⅼ pɘ   │
│ ⊥ʜɘ Ǫnɘɘᴎ oʇ ʜɘɒʁⅼƨ   │
└─────────────────────────────┘

A few props are necessary. On a blank visiting card, copy the code message shown in the illustration. Carry this card with you, along with a transparent glass stirring rod or "swizzle stick" as it is sometimes called. You can buy the rod in a dime store. If you are performing in a bar or anyplace where drinks are being served, you can borrow a stirring rod and forget about your own.

Before starting the trick, hand out for inspection the card with the code message, explaining that you have written a prediction using a new secret government cipher, which you will later decode. After everyone has examined the card, place it aside for a moment.

It is now necessary to force the queen of hearts on a spectator. Any method can be used. I like the following force, originated by Jean Hugard, because it brings a handkerchief into the presentation, and additional props always add variety and interest to card magic.

The queen must be on top of the deck before the trick begins. False-shuffle the cards to retain the queen's position, then borrow a handkerchief and place the deck under it. As soon as the deck is out of sight, turn it over so that it lies face up in the palm of the left hand. The handkerchief is draped over it and the audience believes it to be right side up.

Ask someone to grasp the deck through the cloth and lift up a portion of the cards as if he were cutting the pack. As soon as this is done, the left hand reverses the half that it holds (concealed by the handkerchief, of course) and immediately places it face down on the table. Everything looks very fair, and the audience believes the top card of the half on the table to be the card below the break made by the spectator's cut. The card is, of course, the queen of hearts.

To strengthen the illusion of a fair cut, take the handkerchief from the spectator, holding the cards through the cloth, and with the other hand reach underneath and remove the half that remains. Turn it over also just before bringing it into view, and place it aside on the table.

Tap the back of the queen with your finger and call attention to the fact that this is the card to which the spectator cut, and that it is also the card mentioned in the code prediction.

Turn over the queen of hearts.

Pick up the code message and tell the audience that the code is kept very secret by the U.S. Army and that to divulge the key would be to make public a secret of great value to enemies. However, you add, you will be glad to *translate* the code for them.

Pretend to do this, reading very slowly, as if with difficulty, "Your selected card will be the queen of hearts." Naturally, this stratagem will bring expressions of dissatisfaction from the audience. How do *they* know that is what the code says?

Finally you agree to let them in on the secret of the code. Speak in hushed tones, as if you were revealing dangerous information. Bring the swizzle stick from your pocket and polish it briskly with the handkerchief, explaining that the glass rod has peculiar optical properties and that only a person possessing such a rod can read messages written in the cipher.

Hand the rod and the code message to the audience, asking them to read the code *through* the rod by holding the rod about a quarter of an inch above the writing.

When they do this they will find that the rod automatically decodes the cipher, and the prediction, "Your selected card will be the queen of hearts," jumps into view.

A NEW FALSE CUT

I worked out this cut a good many years ago. I believe I was the first to describe it in print. To explain it, first I will describe the way in which the cut is executed fairly.

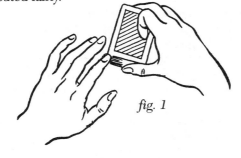

fig. 1

The deck is held in the right hand as shown in figure 1. The tip of the left forefinger rests on the corner. The left hand moves forward, the tip of the finger swinging the upper half of the deck with it, bringing the cards to the position in figure 2. The upper half is now allowed to fall into the palm of the left hand, and the right hand places its half on top. The cut is fair, and it makes a neat flourish when done rapidly and smoothly. I think Jimmy Thompson was the first card performer I saw cut the deck in this manner. It was also one of Nate Leipzig's favorite flourishes.

To make the false cut, follow the above moves to the point at which the upper half drops into the palm of the left hand. Instead of the right hand placing its half on top, it moves *over* the left hand and places the cards on the table. The left hand remains stationary. The right now returns and takes the cards from the left, placing them on top of the cards on the table.

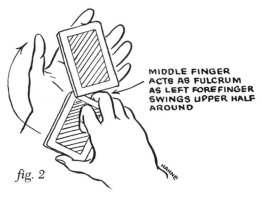

MIDDLE FINGER
ACTS AS FULCRUM
AS LEFT FOREFINGER
SWINGS UPPER HALF
AROUND

fig. 2

The cut looks very fair from all angles, but actually replaces the deck in its original order.

A MIRACLE—MAYBE

This is one of those tricks in which a miracle may occur if you get a lucky break. Otherwise, you do a good trick anyway. Joe Berg of Chicago figured it out and was kind enough to let me use it.

Fan the deck for a selection, but ask the spectator *not* to look at the card. Instead, ask him to mark the back of the card with a pencil, marking it any way he wishes. The card is returned to the deck, which is then shuffled by the spectator.

It is necessary for you to know the name of the card. If you wish, you can force the card. Or, if you prefer, have the card replaced and get a glimpse of it by your favorite method. I usually have the card inserted into a fan in such a way that the lower left corner of the card projects from the fan. After the fan is closed, this corner projects slightly in back and the index can be glimpsed as the deck is squared and handed out for a shuffle.

After the shuffle, spread the deck face up on the table. As you arrange the spread, find the selected card and expose it slightly more than the other cards. Then, to throw the spectator off his guard, spread the cards at some other point so that another card is *even more exposed*. (If the chosen card is near either end of the spread, it is a good plan to shift the cards about as if mixing them, then arrange the spread with the chosen card nearer the center.)

Ask the spectator to look over the cards and name any one he wishes. There is just a chance that he will avoid the obviously exposed card and pick the chosen card, which is slightly less exposed. If he does—then you have the miracle. Merely slide the card forward and turn it over to reveal it to be the one originally chosen and marked.

If he names some other card, you have an ingenious "out." Slide the card he named slightly forward, and note how many cards it is away from the one originally selected. You now must devise some method of counting from one card over to the other. Since no one knows what you intend to do, any method of counting will seem legitimate.

There are many different ways of making this count. For example, you can spell the name of the card. Or you can spell the name with the addition of the word "the." Or you can spell just the value of the card. Or you can spell only the suit. Or you can abandon spelling entirely and use the value of the card for counting (for example, if it is the nine of spades, you can count over nine cards). Remember that in all these cases you have a leeway of three cards. That is:

1. You can begin the count (or spelling) on the card that you slid forward, and end the count on the originally chosen card.

2. You can begin on the card, finish the count, then take the next card.

3. You can ignore the card slid forward, beginning your count on the next card, and then, after the count, take the next card also.

Since you have arranged the spread with the marked card near the center, and since the spectator usually will choose a card near the center, you are not likely to have very many cards separating the two selected cards. And there are so many ways that the count can be made, you are almost certain to be able to terminate the effect in a convincing manner.

If the card named by the spectator is next to the originally selected one, on either side, you can reverse the card named, square the deck, and command the two cards to come together.

Another "out" that can be fallen back upon in difficult cases is to cut the deck at the point indicated by the card named, then deal the cards from either the top or bottom (depending upon whether the selected card is near the top or bottom of the deck) until the spectator says "Stop." If you remember how far the card is from top or bottom you can deal until you come to the card, then hold it back either by dealing seconds (if you are dealing from the top of the deck) or by the "glide" (if you are dealing from the bottom) until you are commanded to stop.

After a few trials you will soon acquire the knack of working out the best solution for a given situation.

A FACE-TO-FACE ROUTINE

White-border cards are necessary. The trick begins with the selection of a card, which is then brought to the bottom of the deck by any method you wish. The bottom three cards then must be secretly reversed. (The reader is referred to the trick "Face-to-Face Fantasy," described earlier, where I explain a way of doing this with two bottom cards while you are apparently explaining what you intend to do in the trick. The method is applicable here.)

After the cards are reversed on the bottom, the deck is cut in the center and the Tenkai move is executed, apparently placing the two halves face to face. (For the Tenkai move, see the trick just mentioned.)

Hold the deck squared in the left hand, with the three reversed cards on top. Spread the two top cards slightly to show the back of the top three cards, calling attention to the fact that the cards in the upper half of the pack are facing downward.

Square the deck again, and with the left thumb riffle the left edge of the pack, beginning the riffle in the center and moving downward to expose the faces of the lower half. Call attention to the fact that the cards in the lower half are all facing upward. If you wish, at this point you can turn the deck over twice to strengthen the illusion that the two halves are actually face to face.

Explain that to cause all the cards to face the same way again, it is only necessary to reverse a single card. Make a double lift of the top two cards, turning them as a single card face up on the deck. Immediately remove the top card (keeping the pack carefully squared in the left hand) and insert it into the center of the deck. This exposes the face-up card beneath.

To prove that all the cards are now face up, fan the deck, keeping the top few cards close together so as not to expose the second card from the top, which is still reversed. Give the deck a cut, ask for the name of the chosen card, then spread the cards face down on the table. The selected card will be reversed in the center of the spread.

TACK IT

Johnny Paul gave me this one. Probably every magician (especially those from Chicago) has heard of Johnny Paul. Johnny was a "fixture" at the

Gay Nineties bar, in the La Salle Hotel, perfecting his own original and amazing brand of bar magic. The customers loved it.

A card is selected and returned to the deck. The deck is shuffled and placed in the card case, which is shown freely on all sides. Johnny then slaps the case against the wall behind the bar and the card suddenly appears on the wall, fastened securely with a thumbtack!

Before the trick begins, Johnny inserts a thumbtack into the bottom of the card case. The selected card is brought to the top. After the deck is shoved into the case, the right fingers secure the tack and palm it as shown in figure 1.

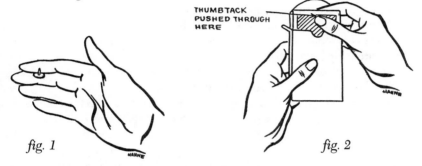

THUMBTACK PUSHED THROUGH HERE

fig. 1 *fig. 2*

Under cover of the flap, the right thumb pulls up the top (selected) card slightly, as in figure 2, and the tack is pushed through the card as shown. The left hand closes the case, pushing the flap between the card and the deck. This leaves a portion of the card, with the thumbtack, exposed as in figure 3.

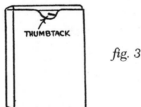

THUMBTACK

fig. 3

The case is shown on all sides by holding it at the top between the thumb and fingers, with the fingers covering the tack. It only remains to slap the case against the wall, then quickly lower it to free the card.

Another way of getting the tack into the card is to hold it by clipping the point between the tips of the first and second fingers. With these fingers, push the flap down between the card and the pack, leaving the tack wedged between the flap and card. The thumb and fingers of the right hand then grasp the upper end of the case, with the fingers on either side of the tack. Slap the case smartly on the left hand. Under cover of this noise, the fingers push the card against the tack so that it penetrates the card.

The best method of handling this part of the effect, however, will naturally depend on the conditions under which you are working.

UNIFORMED SERVICES

This snappy and patriotic effect can be done with anybody's deck. It does require, however, the use of a "stranger card."

Shop around in discount stores until you find three decks of picture-backed cards—one deck with a soldier on the back, another with a sailor (or a battleship), and another with an aviator (or an airplane). Take a single card (any card) from each deck and carry the three in your pocket until an occasion for performing the trick arises, such as when you are working a party date and someone in military uniform is in the audience. Let's assume the person is in the navy. Secure the card with the sailor picture and place it, unknown to the audience, on the bottom of the deck.

Riffle-shuffle, keeping the "stranger card" on the bottom. Then begin a Hindu Shuffle, pulling the packets from the top of the deck with the left hand. Turn to the sailor and ask him to tell you to stop at any time he wishes. When he does so, hold up the packet remaining in the right hand, exposing the bottom card (which is the stranger card). Ask him to remember the card. Place the packet on top of the cards in the left hand and square the deck. State that you will endeavor to locate his card without looking at the face of a single card.

Hold up the cards, faces to the audience, and begin fanning them from left to right. When you come to the stranger card, push it up several inches out of the fan. Ask him if that is his card. When he says it is, ask if he knows how you were able to locate it so quickly.

He won't know. Turn the cards around to show the backs and say, "It was easy—your card is the only one that has a sailor on it!"

The trick is handled the same way, of course, for a soldier or an aviator. There are many other tricks that can be worked with other types of picture cards. For example, you can find decks with a baby or an old man with whiskers on the back.

You can let the spectator keep his card for a souvenir, because you have enough cards to do the trick fifty-two times.

A CURIOUS CARD VANISH

A card is made to vanish from beneath a handkerchief and reappear reversed in the center of the deck. If you wish, you can have the card selected and marked for later identification before beginning the effect.

Follow the illustrations carefully. The deck and handkerchief are held in the left hand as shown in figure 1. The right hand holds the card as shown in figure 2, with the face of the card to the audience.

fig. 2

fig. 1

Keep the left hand stationary and bring the right hand behind the cloth. As soon as it is hidden from the audience, extend the first and second fingers as shown in figure 3. The third and fourth fingers clip the card and bend backward.

fig. 3

The right hand now moves forward, the extended fingers lifting the cloth at the center to give the appearance that a card is beneath it (figure 4). This brings the deck immediately over the card. It is a simple matter to pick it up with the left thumb so that it goes on the bottom of the deck, reversed. The entire sequence of moves should be made smoothly and quickly. It should appear as if you merely placed the card beneath the handkerchief and by means of it lifted the cloth from the left hand.

fig. 4

After the card has been picked up by the left hand, place the deck face down on the table, with the reversed card on the bottom. State that you will cause the card under the handkerchief to vanish.

With the left hand, jerk away the cloth suddenly, at the same time bringing your right fingers to the position shown in figure 5, as if they had been holding the card. Show the cloth and both hands freely to prove that the card is gone.

fig. 5

Pick up the deck and, as you bring it forward, execute a pass, placing the reversed card in the center. Fan the deck with the backs of the cards to the audience until you come to the card.

To enhance this effect, after placing the deck on the table, pretend to pick up the card through the cloth with your left hand. (To prevent the cloth from sagging between your right two fingers, grip the right end of the supposed card between the tips of your left hand's first two fingers, and grip the left end of the supposed card between your thumb and third finger. Stretching the cloth keeps the edge sharp, giving a strong illusion of a card under the handkerchief.) Then let go with your left hand, as your right hand whisks away the handkerchief and gives it a shake.

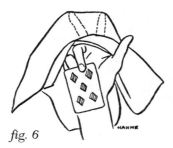

fig. 6

Another, and perhaps even more startling, adaptation of this same sleight is the following effect, in which a card appears to penetrate a handkerchief. Hold the card by the end instead of the side, and place it behind the handkerchief as before. The left hand does not hold the deck; it merely holds the cloth at the center of one edge. The right third and fourth fingers clip the card and bend it backward, while the first and second fingers are extended—this time not so far apart, as the card is held vertically—to pick up the cloth. Drape the back edge of the handkerchief over the thumb and the third and fourth fingers as shown in figure 6, instead of letting the edge hang down over the entire hand.

The right thumb now presses against the end of the card, bending it as shown in figure 7. Release the card from the thumb, at the same time raising the third and fourth fingers.

The audience will see the card snap suddenly into view (figure 8) as if it had jumped upward through the center of the cloth!

fig. 8

fig. 7

X-RAY TOUCH

A combination of old principles makes this trick as baffling to most magicians as to a lay audience. The magician keeps cutting the deck and naming the top card after touching it with the tip of his finger. The more often the trick is repeated, the more confusing it becomes.

fig. 2

fig. 1

Have someone shuffle the deck and hand it to you. Hold it in the left hand as shown in figure 1. With the right, cut off a portion of the deck and place it on the table. Explain that by touching the top of the packet on the table you will be able to name the top card immediately. As you say this, turn your left hand over and place the tip of the index finger on the packet as shown in figure 2. As the hand turns, the third and fourth fingers push on the lower end of the top card. This jogs the end of the card to the right as shown, exposing the index corner slightly. The exposed corner is completely concealed from the spectators by the left hand.

As the left hand turns back to its original position the cards are automatically squared. Place the packet in the left hand atop the cards on the table and square the deck. You have explained what you intend to do and at the same time obtained a glimpse of the top card of the deck.

Repeat the process of cutting, exactly as before, but this time name the card when you touch it. At the same instant obtain a glimpse of the card on top of the packet in the left hand. You are now set to repeat the trick. In other words, by working "one ahead" of the audience—obtaining the name of the "next" card at the same moment that you touch and name the last one—you can repeat the effect as often as you wish.

I find it best to do the trick rapidly about five or six times, then go on to another effect and leave them guessing. A neat way to finish the effect is to glimpse the top *two* cards instead of one. You can do this by applying a little more pressure as you slide the top card, so that the second card slides a trifle also and the indices of both cards come into view. Then, instead of making a fair cut, make a slip cut (as described in "The Unconfused Joker") and place each half on the table. Since you know the top card of each half, you can place the index finger of the left hand on one packet and name the top card, then place the index finger of the right hand on the other packet and name that card also.

ROTATING KNIFE

Place a table knife flat on the hard surface of a table, and put a fork on it as shown (figure 1). Move the fork back and forth until the knife is balanced on the raised portion in the center where the handle joins the blade. A slight push will start the knife and fork rotating like a carnival spindle.

If you do the trick in which a mechanical bird finds the selected card in a circle of cards surrounding him, you'll find that the rotating knife provides a convenient impromptu method of doing this beautiful effect. The handling is as follows:

On top of the deck, have thirteen cards of one suit, say spades, arranged in order from ace on top to king. False-shuffle, holding this stock.

fig. 1   *fig. 2*

Spread the cards for a selection near the center. The card is placed on top of the spread; the deck is squared and cut several times. Form the cards into a complete circle by spreading them clockwise until the ends join. Place the knife and fork in the center (figure 2).

Let the spectator give the knife a spin. When it comes to rest, turn over the card to which the knife points. Whatever the pips indicate, count that number of cards around the circle, tapping clockwise. Turn over the card to which you count. Once again, count the number of cards indicated by the face. Continue counting and turning cards until you turn over a spade.

At this point, announce that the next card will be the selected one. Because of the setup, the count will always end on the chosen card.

Part 2. MATCHES

WOODEN MATCHES

MAGNETIZED MATCHES

A matchbox is shown to be half filled with matches, then closed and turned upside down. The drawer is removed, still inverted, but the matches do not fall. It is shaken slightly and the matches are heard to rattle. The drawer is now pushed back into the cover and out the other side, whereupon the matches drop out immediately on the table. The trick is prepared for beforehand by breaking a match to the proper length so that it can be wedged crossways in the center of the drawer. In removing the drawer your fingers press the sides and hold the piece of match in place. This prevents the matches from falling. When the drawer is pushed out the second time, your fingers do not press the sides so the matches drop to the table and bury the smaller piece.

ESCAPO

This trick first appeared in print in Tom Seller's *Tricks That Work*. A matchbox is placed on the open palm of the left hand and tapped lightly. When the box is lifted a match is found resting on the palm. Before showing the trick, push a match between the cover and the bottom of the drawer. Show the box and hands freely, then remove the drawer and raise the cover up so that the audience can look through it. The tip of your right middle finger holds the match against the bottom of the drawer, where it cannot be seen (see illustration on next page). When the drawer is replaced, the match, still held by the tip of the finger, goes outside instead of inside the cover. The completion of the trick is apparent.

54

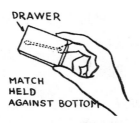

DRAWER

MATCH
HELD
AGAINST BOTTOM

STRIKING EN PASSANT

Secretly place a few coins in the end of a matchbox to give it weight. Toss it into the air, spinning it end over end like a wheel, and jab a match upward at the sides as it falls. With a little practice you should be able to light the match nearly every time.

MATCHBOX MONTE

Three matchboxes, two empty and one half-filled, are placed on the table. They are moved about rapidly and the audience is asked to point to the box containing the matches. They are wrong every time. Actually you use a fourth box, also half-filled, but it is concealed up your right sleeve, where it is held against the arm with a rubber band. When you begin the trick, you pick up an empty box with your right hand and shake it. The rattle from the hidden box seems to come from the box in your hand, and the audience will believe it to be the box containing the matches. Shift the boxes about and ask them to point to the filled one. They are wrong, of course, as you can prove to them by shaking all the boxes with your left hand. Work out other variations to suit yourself.

MATCH AND HANDKERCHIEF

Old but still good. A match is previously pushed into the hem of a handkerchief. A second match (the only one the audience sees) is placed under the handkerchief and someone is asked to hold it through the cloth. Actually the person is given the match in the hem while you carry the other match away concealed in your hand, and pocket it. The vanish is effected by shaking the handkerchief open. A second version is to leave the match in the handkerchief and have the spectator break the one he is holding. When the handkerchief is opened the match is found to be restored.

ANOTHER METHOD

This will fool those who know the older trick. The extra match is not placed in the hem, but in your pocket. The handkerchief is spread over your thigh (your foot is resting on the seat of a chair) so that the match in the pocket is just beneath the center of the handkerchief. Another match is shown and placed under the cloth, but it is the match in the pocket that someone is asked to hold with a finger or to break. At the conclusion the handkerchief can be examined.

STILL ANOTHER METHOD

In this version the extra match is concealed in the end of the magician's necktie. He must perform without a jacket, or with his jacket open and no vest. The handkerchief is held close to the body, and when the match is placed beneath it, the end of the tie secretly is brought up under it also. It is this match in the tie that someone takes through the cloth. When the handkerchief is shaken, the tie drops down unnoticed.

AND STILL ANOTHER

This idea is found in Osborne and Bailey's *Wrinkles*. You wrap a match in a handkerchief and break it several times, yet when the handkerchief is unrolled the match is found whole. No extra matches are used. The secret is that you do not break the match completely but merely bend it until it snaps. You then bend the match straight again before you open the handkerchief. The breaks will not be visible even at close range. Some matches work better than others.

ELECTRIC MATCH

A match is laid across the open palm of the left hand (fingers pointing ahead) so that the head projects over the right side. A second match is "charged" by rubbing it on the magician's clothing, and is then brought up to the other match so that its head is just beneath the head of the match on the palm. The match in the right hand is pointing away from the magician. As soon as the heads touch the match on the palm flies several feet into the air. The trick is accomplished by secretly snapping the lower end of the match held in the hand. The snap is made by the fingernail (or fingertip) of the second or third finger. The nail catches the lower end of the match, applies pressure upward, then slips off suddenly. The magician's right side should be slightly facing the audience.

INVISIBLE HAIR

A match is allowed to burn halfway (hold it vertically while it burns in order to make the carbon more brittle). It is held upright by the lower end while you pretend to take a long hair in your other hand and to wrap one end of it around the burned head of the match. Pretend to take the loose end of the hair and jerk it suddenly toward yourself. At the same time give the match the "snap" (as in the previous trick), and the burned head will flip off exactly as if a hair had actually jerked it.

BLOWING THROUGH THE SLEEVES

A lit match is held in one hand. When you blow down the other sleeve the flame goes out. The real cause is the "snap" (as in "Electric Match"), which is made vigorously enough to put out the flame. A nice variation is to light a cigarette and hold it in one hand and the lit match in the other. Blow on the cigarette and at the same time snap out the match.

VANISHING PENNY

A penny is spun on a plate and then hit suddenly with the flat side of an empty matchbox. The penny vanishes and is found under the plate. A second penny is previously placed under the plate. When the spinning penny is struck, it is driven through the box to the inside.

FLY-APART MATCHES

Two matches are placed on the table about an inch apart. When you draw your finger between the matches, they roll away in opposite directions. Secret: blow gently between the matches. If you pretend to charge your finger electrically by rubbing it on the back of your head, it will be a good excuse to lower your head and bring your mouth closer to the table.

ODD AND EVEN

Someone's hands are placed, palms down, on the table and fifteen matches are placed between the fingers as shown on the next page. One at a time, the pairs are removed and separated, one match being placed to the left, and the other to the right. When you have finished with the pairs there will be two piles on the table. Explain that since the matches were in pairs, each pile must contain an even number of matches. Have someone point to a pile and add the remaining match to the one chosen, apparently making that pile now contain an *odd* number of matches. You state that you will cause the piles to change places. When each is counted, this seems to have occurred. The secret lies in the fact that you separated seven pairs so that each pile actually contains seven matches, an odd and not an even number. Adding the extra match really made the pile even. Note: Count the piles by picking the matches up quickly by pairs. Do not count them by number.

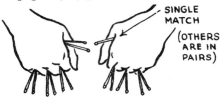

SINGLE MATCH
(OTHERS ARE IN PAIRS)

TRAMPS AND GEESE

This trick is very old. Five matches are placed on the table and two additional ones are taken, one in each hand. The five matches represent geese; the other two represent tramps who plan to steal the geese. You illustrate the stealing by picking up the five matches one at a time, alternating hands in doing so. Continue the story by saying that the tramps see the farmer coming, so they quickly replace the geese (lay the five matches down, alternating hands). When the farmer has gone they again take the geese (again pick up the matches, alternating hands). Now the tramp on the left begins to complain because he has only one goose, whereas his partner has four. Open the hands and show that, indeed, each hand contains one match representing a tramp, while the left hand has only one other match and the right hand has four more. The trick is self-working. Begin by picking up the matches with the right hand, but begin laying them down with the left. This really leaves the left hand empty, but keep it cramped, as if it contained a match. Pick them up the second time beginning with the right hand, and that's all there is to it.

WHICH HAND?

A match is placed on the table and the left hand is laid flat over it, palm up, and with the fingers pointing toward the right (see illustration on next page). A second match is on the table, head pointing away from you, about a foot to the right. This second match is picked up by the right hand and placed in the left hand, which closes over it, exposing the match beneath. The match on the table is now picked up by the right hand and the hands are separated. The left hand makes a throwing motion to the right. Naturally, the match rolls out. This routine is now repeated, but to everyone's surprise, when the left hand makes the throwing motion, nothing rolls out. Instead, the right hand opens and rolls out both matches. The trick is repeated indefinitely. The sleight is simple but the misdirection is perfect. The first routine is merely a buildup. On the second trial the moves must appear exactly the same, but instead of taking the match in the left hand, you retain it in the right while the left hand closes without it. The right hand now picks up the other match and the trick is done. Make the moves slowly and gracefully. Do not make the mistake of *throwing* the match into the left hand. It should be placed there, and the fingers should close over the right hand before it is removed. The best way to hold the match is to take the head between finger and thumb, the stem going back into the palm, and the back of the hand uppermost. The audience should be slightly to your right side.

After you have worked the trick several times, try this for a knockout finish. Instead of placing your left hand over the match, place it flat on the table, and with the right hand pretend to place the match under it. Actually keep the match in the right hand. Then proceed as usual by picking up the match to the right and placing it in the left hand, but this time leave both matches there. As the fingers of the left hand close, reach down to pick up the match on the table and look surprised when you see that it is not there. Open the left hand and roll out the two matches. This is a perfect climax!

MATCH
UNDER HAND

PENETRATING MATCHES

A match is held in each hand, as shown below. When the hands are brought together the matches seem to penetrate each other so that the hands are linked by the matches. They unlink in the same mysterious fashion. Few magicians have bothered to really master this beautiful illusion. The match in the right hand is not held merely between the thumb and finger, but is grasped slightly at one end by the first and second fingers. Thus, when the fingers and thumb are moved apart, the lower end of the match is separated from the thumb. When the hands are brought together, the right hand opens the break just enough to let it by the other match. The motions of linking and unlinking should be more graceful and well-timed than rapid. Hold the matches so that everyone can see exactly what is happening. The trick is described more completely in De Lawrence's *Impromptu Magic*.

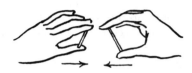

THREE HEAPS

While your back is turned, someone is told to form three heaps of matches on the table, with an equal number of matches in each heap. The number must be more than three. With your back still turned, you state that you will give directions that, if followed, will bring the number of matches in the center heap to any number between one and twelve. The number is chosen and you proceed to accomplish what you have stated. The method is as follows: First, the person is told to take three matches from each end heap and place them in the center. Then the person counts the number in either end heap and removes that number of matches from the center. These are placed on either end. Such a procedure always leaves exactly nine matches in the middle heap. It is now easy to give directions that will bring the center heap to the desired number.

THREE MATCH HEADS

Three match heads are placed on the table. One is placed in the left hand, then another, and the third is placed in a jacket pocket. The left hand opens and out roll three match heads. The trick is repeated several times and finally all the heads vanish. A fourth head is used. It is concealed in the right hand. When the heads are placed in the left hand, the extra head is dropped in also, with either the first or second head. The third head is apparently placed in the pocket, but actually retained in the hand so that the trick is ready for repetition. After working this several times, actually leave the head in the pocket. The next time you merely pretend to place the two heads in the left hand, but really retain both of them in the right hand. Pick up the third head and place them all in the pocket. Show the left hand empty.

MATCH THAT LIGHTS TWICE

Prepare for the trick beforehand by breaking the head from one match and about a fourth of an inch from the bottom of another match. With the aid of a little saliva, stick the head to the bottom of a match so that the join is not visible. Show this match, concealing the real head between the thumb and finger. Light the fake head with the flame of another match and blow it out immediately. Pick up the box with the left hand. Lower your right hand with the match and, as you do so, quickly turn it around and knock off the burned end with the fingers. As your hand comes up, strike the match on the box. The match can now be shown to be quite ordinary.

MUSICAL FORK

The prongs of a table fork are plucked sharply by the fingers of the right hand. The forefinger of the same hand is now lowered inside an empty glass and immediately a musical note is heard. Secret: Concealed in the left hand is an empty matchbox. When you lower the finger, allow the handle of the fork to touch the side of the box (see illustration below), and a note will be heard that will seem to be coming from the glass.

ACROBATIC BOX

Attach a thread to a box as diagrammed below, then tie the loose end to a button on your jacket. Place the box on the back of your hand so that the thread goes forward and through your fingers, then back to the jacket. The box should be resting near the wrist. When you move your hand slowly forward, first the box will move forward, then it will flip over to the other side, and finally the drawer will move out. If the thread is fastened correctly it should pull out of the slit as you hand the box forward for examination. There are more complicated versions of this trick, but this is the simplest and is easiest to prepare.

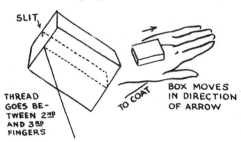

SLIT

THREAD GOES BE-TWEEN 2ND AND 3RD FINGERS

TO COAT

BOX MOVES IN DIRECTION OF ARROW

MATCHES THROUGH THE TABLE

A "feke" is prepared as illustrated below. The box is placed on the table with the feke on top of the end as shown. The box is empty but the feke makes it appear to be half-open and filled with matches. Hit the box with a cupped hand, palming off the feke. It looks as if you knocked the drawer into the box. Reach under the table and leave the feke on your knee, bringing up a handful of matches previously placed there. Then show the box to be empty.

FEKE

HIT HERE

FEKE ON END OF BOX

MYSTERIOUS MARK

With the charred end of a match, a mark is made on the palm of the hand, then the hand is closed. A similar mark is made on the back of the hand and erased with the fingers. The hand is opened and the second mark is seen to be crossing the original one. The secret lies in the fact that the first mark is made to cross diagonally over the upper line of the hand (see illustration below), so that when the hand is closed an imprint is created that looks like a second mark crossing the first one.

MARK ON PALM
MADE HERE

CONTRARY MATCHBOX

This trick, developed by Tom Boyer from an idea in Gamage's magic magazine, is one of the best pocket tricks of all time. Two boxes are used, each of them with the same label on top and bottom. One of these boxes has been prepared beforehand by cutting the drawer in half, turning one of the halves upside down and replacing it, and refilling the drawer with matches. With the aid of this fake drawer you can show the box with the drawer either right side up or inverted, depending on which way you push it out. Now for the working. Give the ordinary box to someone and keep the fake one. Explain that it is impossible for him to manipulate his box exactly as you manipulate yours. You each start with your box half-open. Then you both close your box and go through various routines of turning it first this way and then the other way, while he tries to follow your moves very carefully. Regardless of how well he does so, his drawer is always upside down at the finish while yours is right side up, or vice versa. To bring this about, all you have to do is see to it that in your manipulations you turn the box end over end an odd number of times. You may turn the box any other way that you please, and as many times as you please, but by the time you have finished you must have reversed the ends an uneven number of times. If you wish, you can now put your box in your jacket pocket for a moment as if the trick were over, then on second thought take it out (actually taking out another unprepared box) and ask him if he wishes to examine both boxes.

SHOOTING THE MATCH

J. B. Ward, of Dewsbury, England, sent me this effect shortly after the publication of my book *Match-ic* in 1936. I have never seen it performed by American magicians.

A matchbox is placed on its edge, with one match inserted into the top, and a second leaning against the first as shown. The left hand grasps the box, the thumb pressing against the side nearest you.

Patter about the vertical match representing a soldier behind a trench. With the right hand, take a third match. This represents the gun of an enemy soldier. Place the right hand in front of the matchbox and pretend to "shoot" the soldier in the trench. As you say "bang," the left thumb slides a trifle forward. If the thumb is pressing against the box, this slight and indetectable motion will cause the leaning match to fly suddenly backward! It is the same principle by which "spirit raps" are produced from a pencil.

The effect can be heightened by having the spectator place his forefinger on top of the box to steady it. He will feel a slight tremor as the match flies backward, but the modus operandi will remain a mystery.

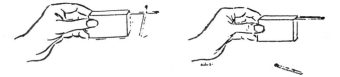

LIGHTING A MATCH TWICE

From time to time various methods of making a match burn twice have been devised. One method is to strike the match, blow it out, then dip the head in water. Under pretense of drying the match, you stroke it through your hair, and in doing so, exchange it for a match previously placed there. This second match is then struck.

A method employing paper matches appeared in one of the magic magazines. With a razor, trim off the sides and top of the head. If this prepared head is struck on the side and quickly blown out, the other side of the head will not ignite. Consequently the match may be struck a second time.

To my mind, however, the most effective method for this trick consists of preparing a handful of wooden matches in advance by covering the heads and a small portion of the stick beneath the head with black ink. You can do this by merely dipping the heads into the ink. Let the matches dry, then carry them in your pocket until you wish to use them.

When you are seated at the table, secretly drop several of these matches into the ashtray. The heads will pick up ash and look exactly like burned matches.

In presenting the effect, first take a genuinely burned match from the tray and attempt to strike it. You are, of course, unsuccessful. Then take one of the prepared matches, and with appropriate patter and hokum, strike it triumphantly.

If you are adept at switching small objects you can present it this way. Have one of the prepared matches finger-palmed in the right hand. Light another match, quickly shake it out, and toss it on the table. Needless to say, as you toss it to the table you retain the match just struck and throw down the faked one. State that as soon as the match cools, you will strike it again. Feel the head of the match gingerly, jerking your fingers away as if it were still warm. Blow on it to cool it more rapidly, then strike it with a flourish.

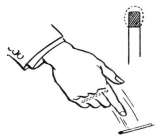

PAPER MATCHES

LIGHT FROM THE WRONG END

Two paper matches are lit, then one is blown out and its head is held just below the lower end of the other match as shown below. It immediately relights. Actually the flame of the upper match travels quickly down the wisp of smoke that rises from the lower match, but it looks as if the match was lit from the lower end. The trick is successful only in a room where the air is quiet.

SMOKE FROM NOWHERE

You light two matches together, shake them out, and then press on your nose with your fingers. To everyone's astonishment a sizable cloud of smoke issues from your mouth. The trick is accomplished by inhaling through your nose the rising fumes from the matches, which are held momentarily below the nose immediately after they are lit.

FOLDER AND STRING

The old ring from string idea can be applied very effectively to paper matches. A hole is punched through a folder and it is threaded on a string held at each end by a spectator. Under cover of a handkerchief the folder is removed unharmed. Secret: A duplicate folder, also with a hole, is concealed in the hand and carried under the handkerchief. The folder on the string is torn off and removed with the handkerchief, revealing the duplicate folder, which has been hung over the string in such a way that it can easily be removed.

REAPPEARING MATCHES

A folder is opened and then closed again so that the matches are outside the flap. The matches are torn away and the flap is placed over the stumps. When the folder is opened again it is filled with matches. Secret: When you close the folder, the flap goes down between the two layers of matches. It is only the front layer that is torn off, the other layer being concealed beneath the flap. When reopened the folder appears to be filled.

DIVINATION

While you are standing with your hands behind your back, have someone hand you a folder of matches. After a moment of concentration, name the firm or product advertised. This clever parlor stunt is a variation of Joe Berg's card-up-the-sleeve idea, explained in *Here's Magic*. Behind your back, you merely place the folder up your right sleeve. Then bring your empty right hand around in front, apparently to rub your forehead. Glance down the sleeve and read whatever is printed on the folder. Needless to say, this process must be reversed before you can return the folder.

PARLOR MIND READING

A dozen or more folders are collected from the audience and placed on a table. While your back is turned, someone is asked to choose a folder, open it, remove a match, close it, and then mix it with the other folders. You are able, by holding each folder to your forehead, to locate the one from which the match was taken. The secret is as simple as the trick is effective. When you gather the folders at the start, you take each of them in hand and, with the thumb, secretly force the flap down very firmly. Later, after someone removes a match, the folder will be closed in an ordinary way. As you raise each folder to your forehead, you feel the flap with your thumb. The folder that is loosely closed is, of course, the selected one.

ONE TO TEN

Prepare beforehand a folder of matches by printing the numbers from one to ten on the heads of ten matches, using a finely sharpened lead pencil. Someone is asked to call out a number between one and ten. You open the folder, tear out the appropriate match, and show it on the unprepared side. Light it and let it burn for some time with the head of the match upward. When you blow out the flame the number will be seen printed in black on a white head. Another use of this same idea is to prepare a match so that it will show the name of a card. Carry the match loose in your pocket until you have occasion to show a card trick. Force the desired card and borrow a folder of matches. Get the prepared match in your hand, open the folder, and pretend to tear out a match, actually showing the prepared one. Strike it, blow it out, and show the name of the selected card.

REMOVABLE HEADS

It is not difficult to hold two matches by the ends, side by side, between the thumb and forefinger and apparently show both sides, actually sliding them between the fingers so that they make an extra turn and show the same side again. This is only one of many tricks utilizing the "slide." Prepare two matches beforehand by scraping off (on one side only) the heads of each. The matches are shown, head side up, and then turned to show the other side, executing the slide so that they appear to be quite unprepared. Pretend to pick off the heads, quickly executing the slide so that the matches now appear headless. Then, with the left hand, pretend to throw the heads back on the matches. As you do so, snap them over quickly to show the head side again.

MATCH-HEAD AMPUTATION

Fred Peterson of New York City created this fine close-up effect. Prepare beforehand by tearing off the head of a paper match and concealing it in the left hand. It should be clipped between the tips of the first and second fingers.

Ask the spectator to extend his right hand, palm up. From a folder, tear a match. Place it on his palm, the head facing to your left. Let it rest there a moment so that he has ample time to inspect it.

With your right hand, pick up the match and make a gesture toward the spectator's left hand. At the same time, ask him to extend his left hand, also palm up. Under cover of the gesture, your fingers rotate the match so that the end now faces the left and the head is concealed by the thumb and finger.

As soon as your hand returns from the gesture, the left fingers immediately take hold of the end of the match and pretend to twist off the head. Actually, of course, the duplicate head is shown. If this move is done properly, the illusion of pulling off the head is perfect.

Drop the head into the spectator's right palm. Your right hand now places the match in his left palm, thumb and finger continuing to conceal the head. Ask him to close his fingers. Take care not to withdraw your finger and thumb until his hand is closed, otherwise he may get a glimpse of the concealed head.

At this point he thinks he is holding a headless match in his left fist, and that the head of this match is resting on his right palm.

Pick up the head, pretend to place it in the left hand, but secretly retain it in the right. Make a throwing motion with your left hand, as if you were throwing the head into his fist. At the same time your right hand allows the match head to drop to the floor.

The head has now vanished. When he opens his left hand, the match is found restored.

DOC ZOLA'S MAGNET ROUTINE

Although a gimmick is required for this trick, the audience never suspects it, and the effect is one of the finest in all table magic. Many magicians know the trick, but few know the details of the routine worked out by the inventor, Doc Zola, of Saginaw, Michigan. It's worth your time to learn Doc's exact routine—the outcome of many hundreds of performances.

First: the preparation. With a razor blade, split a paper match to the head. Break a small piece from the end of a thin needle and insert it between the two halves of the match stem, sticking the point of the needle into the head to hold it in place. Glue the halves together with rubber cement.

The folder is prepared as follows. Remove three matches from the center of the back row. In this space insert a small alnico magnet of the type used as a base for the magnetic pups sold in most novelty stores. A little rubber cement will hold the magnet in place. Stick the prepared match in the front of the folder and your preparation is complete.

Two cards are also used in the trick. They may be playing cards or business cards. Each card is crimped slightly as indicated in figure 1, below.

Begin the routine by taking the folder from your pocket and pretending to tear two matches out of it. One match is actually torn from the folder, but the other, of course, is the prepared one.

Place the two matches on the table in the form of a cross (figure 2). The prepared match is on top. Note that the head of the gimmicked match points to the right, and that the folder—placed to one side—also has the heads pointing to the right. This is important, Doc Zola says, because after a while the needle becomes magnetized. Unless the match and folder are in the proper position, the poles won't match and the magnet won't pick up the needle as well.

Place one of the crimped cards over the cross, convex side uppermost. Put the folder on the center of the card (figure 3).

With the right hand, raise the card a fraction of an inch above the table, the index finger holding the folder in place, while the left hand slides the second card underneath (figure 4). Note that the second card is vertical, and the concave side is uppermost. The cards and folder now appear as in figure 5.

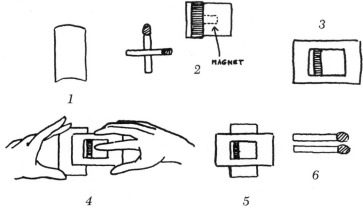

The audience believes both matches to be under the lower card. Actually, the magnet in the folder has caused the top match to adhere to the underside of the upper card. At this point, lift off the upper card, keeping the folder on it with the index finger as before. Say, "As you see, nothing has happened yet." This is important because it convinces the audience that both matches are still under the lower card. Replace the card.

Tap the folder once, then remove it and place it to one side. Take away the upper card to show that a single match has penetrated the lower card.

Offer to repeat, saying that someone may think you hooked the match in some way with the edge of the cards. This time, place the matches side by side as shown in figure 6. Repeat the previous effect, calling attention to the fact that it would be impossible to use the edge of the card for scooping up one match without also scooping up the other one.

The third and last demonstration provides a neat climax. This time form the cross with the prepared match on the *bottom* (and pointing to the right as before). Follow with the same moves. Don't forget to lift away the upper card to show that "nothing's happened yet." Replace the card and tap the folder *twice* instead of once. Remove the folder, then the card, to show that *both* matches have penetrated the lower card!

Put the matches back in the folder and replace it in your pocket. It's a good plan, Doc Zola says, to have in your pocket a duplicate folder with two loose matches in it. You can take this out in case someone wants to try the trick himself.

MATCH PENETRATION 1

Almost every magician knows this old match penetration, which I described earlier with wooden matches. Very few know the correct hand positions for getting the maximum effect when paper matches are used. Properly performed, it's one of the prettiest illusions in impromptu magic.

Moisten the tip of the right index finger and press it against the head of one match until the match sticks to the finger. (The moistened match head will stick more firmly to your finger if you secretly pinch off its tip so that its end is flat instead of rounded.) Hold the two matches as shown in figure 1 on the next page. Note that the match in the left hand is held horizontally, while the other match is vertical. *At no time during the trick does the left hand move.* All motions are made with the right hand. Lift the hand upward and bring it down in a slanting direction as indicated. As soon as it starts downward, the right forefinger is raised slightly, leaving a small opening between the lower end of the match and the thumb—just enough to permit it to pass the other match. Finish as in figure 2. The move is then reversed, bringing the right hand back to its original position.

Remember: The motion of the right hand is not horizontal but slanting. Note the arrow indicating the position of the audience. Unless the audience angle is as shown, the hands will hide the matches.

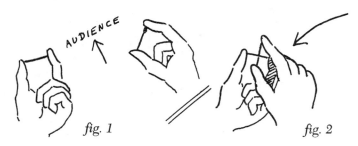

fig. 1   *fig. 2*

MATCH PENETRATION 2

Hold two paper matches by the heads, in the position indicated. Move the hands back and forth for a distance of about six inches, the right hand moving forward as the left moves back, and vice versa. The matches will appear to penetrate each other, though actually, of course, one of them bends back, then springs into place again.

FLOATING MATCH

The magician clasps his hands as shown in figure 1 on the next page. A few inches behind them, apparently suspended in midair, a burning match floats slowly from side to side!

Although the fingers appear to be interlocked in alternating fashion, actually only nine fingers are showing. The middle finger of the right hand projects backward. The burning match is wedged under the fingernail, which supports it in an upright position. Move the finger slowly back and forth to make the match "float."

To finish without revealing the secret, clip the match between the tips of the thumbs, and spread out the hands as shown in figure 2.

A clever variation is to raise the hands in front of the face while holding an unlit cigarette in the lips. Hold the hands a little to one side, then make the burning match float over to light the cigarette.

fig. 1

fig. 2

FOLDER MATHEMATICS

Hand a full folder of matches to someone with the request that, while your back is turned, he tear out a few matches and place them in his pocket. The number must be less than ten. After doing this, he is to count the number of matches that remain in the folder, and to tear from the folder a sufficient number of matches to be able to form that number on the table.

For example, he first tears out five matches and pockets them. This leaves fifteen matches. He then tears out enough matches to form the number fifteen on the table. The number is formed by placing one match to the left, then enough matches in a pile on the right to represent the last digit of the number (1–11111). These matches are also to be placed in the pocket. Once again the spectator tears out some matches. These he holds in his closed fist.

At this point you turn and face the table. One look at the folder and you are able to state the number of matches in his hand.

Secret: Subtract the number in the folder from nine.

COLOR-CHANGING HEADS

This sleight, which I worked out many years ago, later became a popular impromptu stunt with a number of nightclub performers who work tables. A description of the effect appeared in the Winter 1938 issue of the *Jinx*.

At the beginning of the trick, the left hand holds two matches with *blue* heads. The right hand has palmed two matches with *red* heads, concealing them in the manner indicated in figure 1.

State that you intend to pull the heads from the matches in the left hand. The fingers and thumb of the right hand grasp the heads and make an attempt to pull them off. Do this twice. The third time, the fingers of the left hand take the matches from the right hand, and the right fingers carry away the two matches previously held in the left hand. The exchange is a very natural one, and no one is expecting a switch.

After the switch, the matches in the left hand will be upside down. It appears as if the heads have been pulled away. The right hand pretends to toss the heads under the table or to place them in the jacket pocket. This enables you to dispose of the two matches in the right hand.

The rest of the trick is patter and buildup. State that you are going to expose how you did the trick. Of course you didn't really pull off the heads, you explain. Under cover of the right hand, you merely turned the matches upside down, so that their lower ends would be viewed. But— you continue—you never have been able to understand why the trick always causes the heads to change their color. With the right forefinger, rotate the matches around to reveal the red heads. Toss the matches on the table for inspection.

Emphasize at the outset that the heads are blue. Otherwise the audience may forget the original color.

SCIENCE, JOKES, CATCHES

IRON MATCH

Light your cigarette, shake out the match, and calmly toss it to the floor. It hits with a clang! A small nail, finger-palmed in the hand, is thrown down instead of the match. This always gets a laugh.

LIGHTED MATCH FROM BOX

Glue a small piece of striking surface on the upper inside edge of the cover. When you take the match from the box, lever it up against this piece.

SMASH IT

An empty box is placed on the table and the cover is balanced on top of it as shown below. You defy anyone to hit the cover with his fist and smash the drawer beneath. It looks easy, but when he tries it the drawer always flies out from under the cover.

MATCH MUNITION

Arrange three matches on the end of a box as shown below, so that the vertical matches press with considerable force against the ends of the other match. With the flame of a fourth match, light the horizontal match in the center. It will burn a moment and then suddenly it will be shot quite a distance across the room.

NO LIGHT

You hand a lighted match to a friend, but to his surprise he gets only the lower end, while your hand comes away with the light. The match is broken beforehand and held with the break covered by the thumb and finger.

HUMMING MATCH

Hold a match between the thumb and middle finger and toss it into the air, snapping it vigorously so that it has a rapid rotary motion about its lengthwise axis. If snapped hard enough it will give forth an audible tone.

STRENGTH TESTER

It looks easy, but a match held as shown below is impossible to break, using the strength of the fingers alone.

WALKING MATCH

A large kitchen match is bent and placed over a table knife, held by someone as illustrated below, so that the ends of the match touch the table. The arm must not rest on the table. Unless the person's hand is very steady it will jiggle slightly and cause the match to walk slowly along the edge of the knife.

VANISHING MATCHES

Bend back slightly the striking flap of a folder and with a sharp knife sever both layers of matches, cutting just above the staple. Glue the two layers at the base. When they are replaced in the folder everything will look unprepared. The next time a friend wants a light, produce this prepared folder, tear out a match for yourself (letting him see that the folder is well filled), close it, and tilt it sideways in your hand before you hand it to him.

The matches will drop into your palm. When he takes the folder and opens it he will find it empty.

POP-UP

Make a small hole on the top of a box near the end of the cover and push a match through it so that only the head remains outside. When you open the box by shoving the drawer forward, the match will push out of the hole into an upright position.

MATCH-HEAD SUBMARINES

Break off the head of a large kitchen match, place it in a bottle filled with water, and put in the cork. You will find that by pressing hard on the cork you will be able to cause the head to sink to the bottom, and loosening the cork will cause the head to rise. Adjust the cork so that the head is just ready to sink. By holding the bottle by the sides and squeezing it, you can make the head rise or sink at pleasure and no one will know the cause. Different heads rise and sink at different pressures, so you can put in several heads and make them perform one at a time.

PROLONGED KISS

Punch a small hole in the top of a box and stand a match upright in it, with the match head at the top. Place a second match on top of the box, leaning it up against the fixed one so that the heads touch. Now light the leaning match in the center. Soon the heads will light (which represents the kiss), and as the flame continues to burn, the free match will be raised slowly off its "feet" as it curls upward into the air.

LIGHT FOR TWO

Prepare a paper match by pulling it apart at the lower end and splitting it in half up to the head. Hold the match so that it looks quite unprepared, light it, and when the head burns past the break, slide the thumb and finger so that the two pieces fan out. It looks as if one match suddenly became two.

ROLY-POLY BOX

Bend an empty folder slightly as shown below and place it on the table in the position indicated at the right of the drawing. The fingers raise the lower edge until the folder overbalances. Because of the heavy lower end, it will turn a complete somersault.

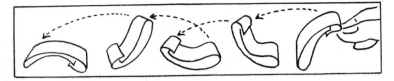

TRICK CIGAR

Stick a match into the end of a cigar so that the head is flush with the cigar's tip. When the victim lights the cigar, the match will cause the end to flare up suddenly. This is a quick way to prepare a harmless joke.

RISING MATCHBOX

Place an empty matchbox on the back of the hand so that the drawer is upside down. Open the box slightly at the end toward the wrist, then close it so that it clips the flesh on the back of the hand. As long as the fingers are extended the box will lie flat, but when you close your hand into a fist, the box suddenly stands on end.

AUTOMATIC LIGHT

The next time you hand a match to a friend, hold the head firmly against the striking surface with the thumb. Extend the end of the match to him. When he takes it, the match will light without injury to your thumb.

OVERSIZE

A wooden match is concealed in the hand. Borrow a folder of paper matches for a light, open it, pretend to tear out a paper match, close it, and strike the wooden match.

STRIKING SAFETY MATCHES WITHOUT THE BOX

Rub the striking surface of the box on whatever surface you wish to use in striking the match—for example, the sole of your shoe, or the top of another matchbox. Enough of the chemical composition will be transferred to make the striking of the match possible. Safety matches will also light when held flat against a pane of glass and drawn rapidly across it.

COVER CHANGE

When you pass your hand over a folder, the cover design changes. Prepare for this trick by cutting off the front side of a flap, cutting exactly at the top so that the upper edge of the severed piece rounds over a bit. Fit this over a folder that has a different design, sticking the lower end of the piece under the striking flap. Show the folder freely and cover it with the palm of your right hand. Palm off the fake cover and pocket it as you hand the folder over for examination. With appropriate designs there is room for interesting patter.

CHIN PENETRATION

A match is previously placed in the mouth so that it can be pushed out easily through the lips with the tongue. A second match is shown at the tips of the fingers and apparently pushed into the chin. Actually it slides back into the hand while at the same time the other match is pushed out through the lips. The effect is sudden and amusing.

ROCKET MATCHES

With the aid of a little tinfoil from a package of cigarettes you can construct a genuine miniature rocket.

Wrap a small piece of foil around the head of a match, but leave a small channel on one side (figure 1). An easy way to make the channel is to place a toothpick against the match until the foil is wrapped, then pull out the pick.

The match folder provides a handy launching platform (figure 2). Be sure the channel side of the foil is underneath. Light another match and hold the flame to the head of the rocket. In a moment the match will ignite and the escaping gas will cause it to zoom across the room.

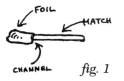

fig. 1

fig. 2

MATCH-FOLDER WAGER

Challenge anyone to strike, one at a time, all twenty matches in a folder. Only one striking attempt is allowed for each match.

The odds are enormously in your favor, because the chemical on the striking surface quickly wears off, making it difficult to strike the last few matches.

It can be done by striking the first ten matches on the right side of the striking surface, then the remaining matches on the left side.

THE NAZI CROSS

Place five matches on the table and ask if anyone knows how to make a Nazi cross with five matches. Stress the fact that the matches must not be broken, and that no more than five are permitted. The answer: Stick four of them in his ear and light them with the fifth!

The idea is old. In a nineteenth-century magic book I found it presented in the form of making a Maltese cross with five matches. The solution began: "First you must procure a native of Malta."

MIKE AND IKE

Fill a soda bottle all the way to the top with water and drop two paper matches inside. If possible, use matches with different colored heads. Let them soak a moment, then place your index finger into the neck of the bottle and press downward. If no air is allowed to escape, the pressure will cause the matches to sink to the bottom of the bottle. To bring them up, insert the finger and create a suction by pulling the finger upward. Releasing the suction sends them back down again.

Since it is unlikely that both matches weigh the same, one match will be the first to go down and last to come back up. Jerry Lukins, of New

York, liked to call one match Mike and the other Ike, then order them up and down singly.

"Okay, Ike, come on back up. That's right. Now, Mike, you follow Ike." And so on.

THE THREE BEARS

A spectator extends his hand, palm up. Three matches are placed upright between his fingers as shown. Concealed in your right fingers is a small sponge that has been dipped in water.

Explain that the matches represent mama bear, papa bear, and baby bear. When they woke up one morning, papa bear was the first to visit the bathroom. As you say this, pick up one of the matches and move it up the spectator's hand until it touches his wrist.

"Then," you continue, "papa bear came back to the bedroom." Move the match back to its original position. Repeat the same moves and patter for mama bear.

Pick up baby bear, the third match, and as you start to move it, say, "But baby bear just couldn't wait," at the same time squeezing a small quantity of water into the spectator's palm.

GRASSHOPPER MATCHES

Split the lower half of the stem of a paper match and fold the two parts as shown in figure 1 on the next page. If the match is held as in figure 2, then quickly released, it will hop into the air.

Two creamers can be stacked upside down as shown in figure 3, and the match made to jump from the top creamer into a glass.

Another, even more ridiculous, way to make matches hop is to bend the left arm as in figure 4. Place the match against one of the folds of cloth, press down, and release quickly. The fold acts as a springboard, sending the match several feet into the air.

The only table stunt I know sillier than this is to break little bits off a wooden toothpick and stick them around on the face (figure 5). A slight pressure of the broken ends against the skin causes the pieces to stay in place.

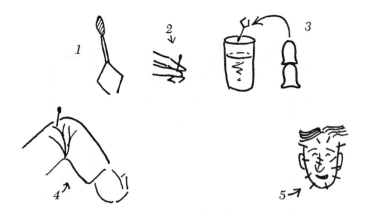

BLOWING OUT THE MATCH

Here are four amusing ways to puff out the match after you light a cigarette.

1. Hold it above the head and pretend to blow forward. Actually, stick out your lower lip and blow upward. With a little practice you can blow it out every time. The eyes of the audience follow the match as you raise it. No one notes the projecting lip.

2. Pick up a glass, keeping the burning match in your fingers (figure 1, on the next page). Pretend to blow through the glass. The match will go out.

3. Hold the burning match in the right hand and extend the hand to the side. At the same time, bend the match as shown (figure 2). Raise your left hand and blow down the left sleeve. At this instant the fingers of the right hand cause the match to rotate quickly. This is done by sliding the thumb forward. The sudden rotation will snuff out the flame.

Bert Allerton has combined this principle with another match stunt. He holds the two burning matches as shown in figure 3. The match in the right hand is bent and ready to be snapped out. As soon as it goes out, the rising plume of smoke passes the flame of the other match, and the lower one immediately ignites again. Actually, the flame travels quickly down the smoke. The effect is startling. With no apparent movement of the hands, the lower match goes out, then ignites again!

4. Hold the flame about six inches from the lips. Say, "Little Bo Peep."

MATCH, NICKEL, AND GLASS

Balance a nickel on its edge, then balance a paper match on the edge of the nickel. Cover it with a glass as shown.

The problem is to make the match fall off the nickel. You are not permitted to shake the table or touch the glass in any way.

Solution: Run a pocket comb through your hair several times to charge it with electricity. Hold the comb against the side of the glass. The match will fall.

GLASS AND CHECK

Place a restaurant check, or dollar bill, under a glass and balance a coin on the rim of the glass as shown. Problem: Remove the check without touching the glass with anything not already touching it, and without dislodging the coin. In addition, the check cannot be jerked, but must be removed slowly.

Solution: Roll the end of the check until the roll touches the glass. As you continue to roll it by the ends, the center of the roll will push the glass off the check.

HAPPY BIRTHDAY

Here's another practical joke with matches that never fails to get a laugh. Have the victim form his hand into a fist. Place three matches between the fingers as shown. Light them with another match. After they've burned a moment, ask the victim to blow them out in one puff.

As soon as he blows them out, begin to sing, "Happy Birthday to You." Better yet, tip the others off in advance so that the entire table can burst into song.

HAVE A LIGHT

The next time you light a friend's cigarette, try this. Moisten the end of the match. Strike it, then extend the finger as shown. The match will remain balanced! You can hold it to the friend's cigarette, then blow it out while it is still standing.

Another funny and surprising way to offer a light is to strike the match behind your ear. The preparation is easy—just cut a small rectangle from the striking surface of a folder, and stick it behind the ear with a little wax.

KIDDIE KAR

Split one match near the head and push another match through the opening to make a cross (figure 1, on the next page). Hand it to a victim (the larger he is, the funnier it will be later) and have him hold the matches as shown in figure 2. Ask him to shuffle his feet on the floor to generate static electricity. Assure him the matches will not ignite and burn his fingers. After he has shuffled his feet a while, slap him on the back and ask, "How do you like your new kiddie kar?"

CROSS OF PEPPER

Little Johnny Jones gave me this unusual table stunt. Prepare for it in advance by pushing the lower end of a paper match into your ear to pick up a little earwax. Go gently—it's easy to damage the eardrum. With the fingers, rub the wax into the lower half of the match. Put the match back into the folder, and carry it with you until you have an opportunity to show the trick.

Sprinkle a liberal quantity of pepper into a glass of water. The grains will form a dark coating over the surface. Challenge everyone to draw a cross on this coating, using the end of a match.

After they've tried and failed, take out your prepared match (pretending to pull it from the folder) and move the waxed end slowly through the water. The pepper grains will separate along the path made by the match. It will be a simple matter to form a cross of clear water against the black background of the pepper.

PUZZLES

PERFECT SQUARE

Place four matches as shown at the left in the drawing. Problem: Move only one match to form a perfect square. (Two methods are shown.)

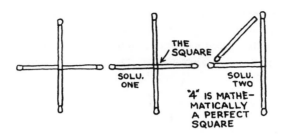

EQUATION

Arrange seven matches as shown in the upper portion of the illustration below. Problem: Move one match and form a balanced algebraic equation. The solution shown is the best. The square root of one is equal to one.

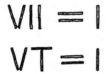

STAR

Four matches are bent and placed as shown below. Problem: Without touching them, form them into a four-pointed star. Solution: Allow a drop of water to fall on the center.

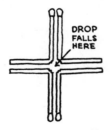

WHAT HAPPENS

Place two matches upright on the end of a box by sticking their ends between the cover and the drawer, as shown on the next page. Balance another match across the heads. The problem is to guess what will happen if the horizontal match is lit in the center. You will get many conflicting replies. Actually the match will burn a moment and then fall off.

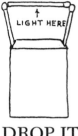

DROP IT

Puzzle: Hold a box of matches vertically about a foot above a table and drop it so that it hits on the end and remains standing upright. Secret: Before dropping the box, see that the drawer projects slightly at the upper end, but keep this concealed by the hand. When you drop the box, the force of the drawer sliding in place will cause the box to remain upright.

CROSSES

Eight matches are placed in a row, as shown below. The problem is to move one match at a time, to either the left or the right, passing it over exactly two matches and laying it across a match to form a cross; and in four such moves to form four crosses. The solution is diagrammed. When the puzzle has been solved or explained, add two more matches to the row and ask someone to try to form five crosses in five moves. Few will realize how simple it is. Merely bring a match fourth from the end over to cross the end match. This leaves eight matches to be solved exactly as before.

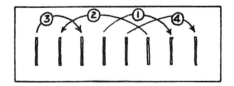

MATCH, TUMBLERS, AND SALT SHAKER

Two tumblers are placed as shown on the next page, with a match supported between them and a salt shaker beneath one of the glasses. Problem: Remove the salt shaker, but the match must not fall and the tumbler not covering the shaker must not be touched. Solution: Light the match (using another match to do so) and quickly blow it out. The head will stick to the tumbler so that the glass covering the shaker may be easily removed without affecting the position of the match. Matches other than safety matches work best.

LINKED HANDS

This old stunt is usually done with corks or chess rooks, but matches work just as well. Grip the centers of two matches in the crotches of each thumb. The hands are brought together so that the finger and thumb of each hand grasp the ends of the match held by the other hand, then the hands are separated. To everyone's surprise they come apart quite easily instead of interlocking as would be supposed. The proper way to twist the hands and grasp the matches is indicated in the drawing below.

PUZZLE LIFT

An empty drawer is placed face down with the cover standing on it as shown below. The problem is to lift both cover and drawer, without touching the drawer in any way. To do this you must grasp the cover with one hand, then bend over and place your mouth over the top of the cover and draw in your breath. The suction will hold the drawer to the cover so that both can be lifted easily.

COVER

DRAWER
INVERTED→

PUZZLE SPLIT

The problem is to split a completely charred paper match exactly in half *lengthwise*. There is only one way to do it. Moisten the balls of each thumb and squeeze the match tightly between them for about a minute, as shown below. When the hands are opened, half of the match will be sticking to each hand.

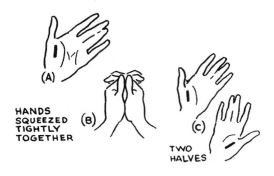

THREE-MATCH PUZZLE

Three matches are placed in a row, with the head of the center match toward you and the heads of the other two matches away from you. The problem is to pick up any pair of matches (one match with each hand) and reverse them, and in three such moves to have them lined up with all the heads pointing *toward* you. Although you demonstrate the solution again and again, others find it impossible to make the moves correctly. Solution: When you work the puzzle you start with the matches lined up as stated. There are several solutions. When you ask other people to try it, you arrange the matches in just the reverse way, with the matches on the end pointing toward them, and the center match pointing away. It will be impossible for them to work the trick no matter how many moves they use.

EASY WHEN YOU KNOW

Problem: Drop a paper match so that it will alight on its edge and remain there. After everyone has tried and failed, you take the match and simply bend it sharply in the middle. No matter how you drop it, it will alight and remain on its edge.

THREE NEW PUZZLES

The following three match or toothpick puzzles have been added especially for this book because they are the best of their kind known to me. It would spoil the fun if I provided answers. See how long it takes for you to solve them!

REVERSE THE FISH

Change the position of three matches to make the fish swim in the opposite direction.

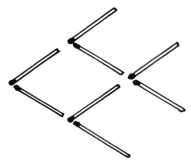

REMOVE THE OLIVE

Change the position of two matches so that the cocktail glass remains the same, but the olive, represented by, say, a dime, is outside the glass. The dime must not be moved. The glass may be in any of the four possible orientations.

DON'T DISTURB THE GIRAFFE

This is best shown with toothpicks, because the match heads play no role in the puzzle. Change the position of just *one* match, but leave the giraffe unaltered. It may, of course, be rotated or reversed. The giraffe's head is made with a small piece of match or toothpick.

Part 3. COINS AND BILLS

VANISHING COIN

To perform this subtle vanish (first shown to me by Joe Berg) you must be resting your chin on your left hand as shown in the drawing.

Hold the coin in your right hand and place your hand in front of you on the table. Ask the person opposite you to cover it with his hand. As he reaches forward, say, "No—I mean the *other* hand." As you say this, draw back your hand (it is a perfectly natural gesture) in such a way that your fingers bring the coin just above the opening of your left sleeve. The person is confused about the changing of hands, so it is a simple matter to drop the coin, unobserved, down the left sleeve!

Place your right hand on the table once more, as if it still held the coin. Have him cover your hand with his. Then ask him to remove his hand. Slowly open your fingers to show that the coin has vanished.

The vanish can, of course, be used for any small object that can be dropped down the sleeve without difficulty.

THE CURIOUS FOLD

The bill is held upright as shown in figure 1, then folded down from the top as in figure 2, and twice to the left as in figures 3 and 4. These moves are now reversed, but when the bill is open once more, it is upside down!

The secret is to make the second fold *backward* as shown in figure 3, and the third fold *forward* as shown in figure 4. When the bill is opened, however, these two folds are both opened from the *front*. This automatically turns the bill upside down.

Unless the spectators have observed you very carefully, they will be unable to duplicate the moves.

In making the folds, the bill should be held at the left side by the left thumb and fingers. The right hand does the folding. If you make the folds rapidly the moves will be more difficult for the spectators to follow.

Do not repeat the trick too often. A good presentation is to cause the bill to turn upside down, then repeat, bring it right side up, and hand it to the spectators to see if they can do it.

SIXTEEN-COIN PUZZLE

Arrange eight pennies and eight nickels on a table, as shown in figure 1 on the next page. Call attention to the fact that in each horizontal row the coins alternate. Problem: Change the arrangement so that each horizontal row will be composed of the same type of coin—that is, two rows of pennies and two rows of nickels. The only stipulation is that you must not touch more than two coins.

Solution: Place the first finger on coin "A" and the second finger on coin "B." Slide the coins to the bottom of the square, to the positions indicated in figure 2, and push up. The result is shown in figure 3.

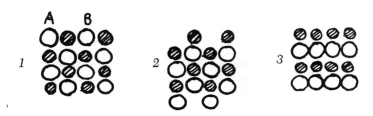

TWO STUNTS WITH A DIME

1. Here's a new "betcha." Can you drop a dime from a height of several inches, making it alight on its edge and remain standing in that position?

Solution: Moisten the side of a glass or bottle with water. Dunk the dime in the water, place it against the side, and drop it. It will slide to the table and remain on edge.

2. Place the dime on the back of the left hand, resting on the first knuckle of the little finger. Snapping the thumb and little finger causes the dime to turn over. No one else can do it. Why? The secret is to snap the thumb away from the finger. Most people do the reverse—they snap the little finger off the thumb.

SPINNING THE HALF-DOLLAR

A half-dollar is placed flat on a table. The problem is to make it spin on its edge without touching it in any way.

Solution: Tear off a portion of a soda straw, about four inches long. Hold it in the position shown and blow vigorously at the edge of the coin. It will begin to vibrate on the table, and if you keep blowing, you'll soon have it spinning. Thanks for this one to Johnny Paul.

SUCKER BET

Take a quarter from your pocket and borrow another quarter from a friend. Place both coins in the center of a table napkin, gather up the ends, and have him hold them. Tap the lower part of the cloth to make the coins rattle. The following dialogue now takes place:

"How many quarters are you holding?"

"Two."

"Are you sure?"

"I'm positive." (If he isn't, let him take a look inside.)

"If you're so sure, will you give me 35¢ for the contents of the napkin?"

If he answers "Yes," ask him for the 35¢. What he forgets, of course, is that one of the coins is his! Actually, he's buying your quarter for 35¢. You'll be surprised at how many smart people fall for this!

PENNY PUZZLE

You need a shiny new penny and a pocket magnifying glass for this one. Hand both items to someone and ask him to tell you how many letters he can find on the face of the penny. The figures in the date do not count as letters.

He'll probably say "19."

The correct answer is "22." If you use the magnifier and look carefully on the left side of the base of Lincoln's bust, you'll find three tiny letters—the initials of the artist who made the engraving.

David Eisendrath, Jr., a New York photographer, called my attention to this.

TRY THIS ON YOUR HAM SANDWICH

Have a half-dollar finger-palmed in the left hand the next time you order a ham sandwich. Lift off the top slice of bread, place it on the left fingers over the half-dollar, then pick up the salt and salt the ham. Replace the bread and turn the entire sandwich over. Unknown to your companions, you have loaded a half-dollar under the ham.

Borrow a half-dollar from someone a few moments later and ask him to remember the date on the coin. Vanish it by the well-known move of tossing it up the left sleeve (or better still, use Joe Berg's clever sleeving method, described in "Vanishing Coin," above). As the right hand picks up the top piece of bread, the left hand lowers, permitting the coin to drop into the fingers. Place the slice on the left hand as before, the half going beneath. The right hand now raises the ham to disclose the coin.

Remove the coin, replace the ham and the upper slice of bread, turn the sandwich over, and repeat the trick. The half-dollar can now be returned. It is the original coin, as can be verified by the date.

COIN THROUGH THE PLATE

For this trick you need a small piece of wax, about half the size of a pea. You can carry it behind a vest button. Before showing the trick, secretly transfer this piece of wax to the underside of a saucer. The center of the underside is usually concave, so the saucer may rest on the table without the wax sticking to the tablecloth.

Borrow a coin, preferably a half-dollar, and a small square of paper. Have the spectator mark the coin for later identification. Wrap the coin in the paper, using the well-known fold that permits the coin to slide into the hand.

Tap the paper on the edge of the plate to prove the coin is still inside, then permit the coin to slide into the left hand. Lower this hand to your lap as your right hand takes the paper and places it on the saucer.

Ask someone to strike a match. While this is being done, hold the saucer in the right hand and bring it to the edge of the table. The left hand comes up from beneath and presses the coin against the wax, causing it to stick to the underside of the saucer.

Place the saucer on top of a glass of water. The spectator sets fire to the paper. As it burns, the heat melts the wax and the coin falls visibly into the glass below.

Retrieve the coin, and dry it with a napkin (this also serves to remove the wax that may have adhered). Return it to the owner for identification.

TESTING A HALF-DOLLAR

This is more of a joke than a trick; it never fails to get a laugh.

Ask your audience if they have seen the new method of testing half-dollars to determine if they are genuine.

Place the half on the table, then grasp an empty tumbler in the manner shown. Strike the half-dollar several times, using the tumbler as a hammer. (The "X" in the drawing labels the portion of the glass that strikes the coin.) It makes a terrific racket, but the tumbler never breaks.

Pick up the half-dollar, saying, "And if the half doesn't break, you know it's not a counterfeit."

Matt Schulien, of Schulien's German restaurant and bar, was the first person I saw present this stunt. The punchline comes from Dorny.

BERLAND'S VANISHING BILL

This fine trick is one of the many remarkable bill inventions of Sam Berland of Chicago.

One bill is prepared in advance by creasing it as shown in figure 1 on the next page. Begin the trick by taking this bill, and an unprepared one, from your billfold. Hold the bills in the left hand, the ordinary bill screening the prepared one. Under cover of the front bill, fold the other one as indicated (figures 2, 3, 4). The unprepared bill is simply folded twice. The two bills now appear exactly alike.

Place the corners of the bills together, holding the corners in your left hand while the right hand adjusts them. Note that the prepared bill is the one nearer you (figure 5).

Under cover of the right hand, the left thumb flips the back fold of the prepared bill from left to right (figure 6). The right hand palms the other bill (figure 7). The left hand now holds only one bill, but because of the peculiar fold, it appears exactly like the two bills that were there before (figure 7). The right hand can either drop the bill on the lap or go to the pocket to take out some object to wave over the bill, leaving the palmed bill in the pocket.

It only remains to grasp the bill by a corner and shake it open quickly. The effect is that of an instantaneous vanish of one of the bills.

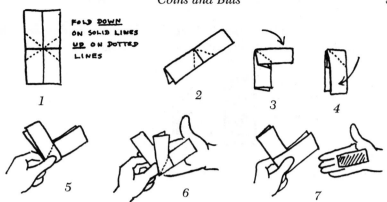

MUSHROOM, KEY, AND STATES

Can you find a mushroom on a dollar bill? It's produced by two horizontal folds as shown. Washington's head becomes the top of the mushroom, his shirt front the stem!

Finding the key on a dollar bill is another tough one. No folding is necessary. The key is in the lower part of the blue seal to the right of Washington's picture.

And did you know that the names of more than twenty states appear on a five-dollar bill? They're in extremely small print, across the top of the Lincoln Memorial. If a glass of water with smooth sides is handy, you can hold the bill flat against the glass and read the names of the states through the water. The curved water acts as a magnifying glass.

VALUABLE PAPER WAD

Fold a five-dollar bill as shown on the next page. The green side is uppermost. Each end is folded as in figure 2, bringing the white spaces together. Then all four sides around the white spaces are folded back until no green shows from above. The astonishing result (figure 3) is a large wad of paper that looks completely blank!

Carry the folded bill in your pocket until an opportune moment occurs, then palm it and pretend to pick it off the floor. Place it on the table and ask your friends if any of them would bother to pick this up if they saw it on the sidewalk. Naturally, they'll shake their heads. Unfold it slowly to reveal the five. Dorny showed me this many years ago.

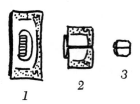

INDESTRUCTIBLE BILL

A diverting bar stunt is to soak a crumpled bill in whiskey or gin, then set fire to it. It will flare up and burn out quickly without damage to the bill.

PAPER TO BILL

Milbourne Christopher is the creator of this simple, beautifully timed switch.

To prepare it, roll a dollar bill into a small ball and have it handy on your lap or in your jacket pocket. Tear off two small pieces of newspaper and hand them to someone across the table with the request that he roll each into a compact ball. While this is being done, your right hand finger-palms the bill.

The two paper balls are placed on the table. Ask the spectator to point to one of them. Pick up the designated ball and casually drop it into the left hand, allowing the palmed ball to fall and retaining the paper. Let the audience get a glimpse of the ball before the left hand closes. The rolled-up bill and the newspaper ball are practically indistinguishable.

The right hand immediately picks up the remaining ball and places it in the pocket, leaving the extra ball there also. "How many balls of paper do I have in my left hand?" you ask.

"One," he says.

"One is correct," you say. Open the hand a moment to show the ball, then close the hand, turn it over, and slap the back of the hand smartly. Roll the ball onto the table, then open it to show that it has changed into a dollar bill.

VANISHING CREAMER

Before you begin this trick a pencil must be in your inside jacket pocket.

With your napkin, clean the inside of an empty creamer (so you won't soil your clothes later), then wrap a dollar bill around it (figure 1). Push the top edges of the bill into the creamer to form a compact cylindrical shell. Take it in the right hand and tap it once or twice against the table.

Reach into your jacket pocket with your left hand to get the pencil. While attention is misdirected to the left hand, bring the right hand to the edge of the table and allow the creamer to drop out of the bill into your lap. Hold the empty bill above the table, with the pencil directly above it (figure 2). Drop the pencil through the bill. Unroll the bill to show that the creamer has vanished. Your left hand can now retrieve the creamer from the lap, come up inside the jacket, and pretend to remove the creamer from the inside pocket.

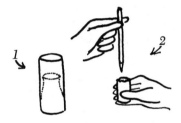

STRIKING A MATCH ON A BILL

Did you know that an ordinary paper match can be ignited by striking it on a dollar bill? Hold the bill flat against a hard surface, and drag the match across it rapidly several times. The tip of the middle finger must press the head of the match firmly against the bill. If you press hard enough, and make the strikes rapidly, the match will ignite after the third or fourth try.

LINCOLN ON TOP

You'll need a five-dollar bill for this one. Bet a friend that if he tosses the bill into the air it will fall to the floor with Lincoln on top. You can't lose! Lincoln's head is on the face of the bill. On the back is a statue of Lincoln in front of his famous monument.

LINKED PAPER CLIPS

Fold a bill into thirds and attach two paper clips as shown. Grasp each end of the bill and pull it flat. You'll be surprised at what happens. The clips will pop off the bill. When you pick them up from the floor they will be linked together!

PUT GEORGE TO SLEEP

Make a horizontal mountain fold that goes through Washington's eyes. Crease it sharply between the nails of your thumb and finger. Unfold the bill. Hold its two ends and tilt it slowly backward. You'll see George slowly close his eyes.

BALANCED HALF-DOLLAR

Crease a bill in half lengthwise, then fold it like a V. Place a half-dollar on it as shown. Believe it or not, if you pull slowly and gently on the ends of the bill to straighten it out, the half-dollar will remain balanced on the creased edge!

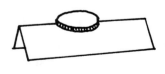

SUPPORT A GLASS

Bet that you can place each end of a crisp dollar bill on the rims of two side-by-side glasses in such a way that the bill will support a third glass on its middle.

The secret: Make five or six sharp pleats in the bill. It will then be rigid enough to support the third glass as shown.

HOW MANY EYES?

Challenge a friend to tell you how many eyes are on a dollar bill. Most people count two eyes on Washington, the eye at the top of the pyramid on the bill's back, and (if they are observant) the eye on the eagle. "No," you say, "the answer is *eight*."

To find the other four eyes, fold the ends of the bill as shown to make two bug-eyed green monsters.

PSYCHIC MOTOR

Bend open a large paper clip as shown to make a stand on which to balance a dollar bill. The bill is creased in half both ways with mountain folds, then opened flat. It will balance on the top end of the paper clip. You have made a psychic motor!

Hold your hand on one side of the bill, as shown in the drawing on the next page. In your mind, command the bill to rotate. Sure enough, in a few moments it will start to turn! Of course, your mind has nothing to do with it. Heat from your hand produces a current of air that moves the bill. Even without your hand, the bill may start rotating as a result of your breathing or from slight air currents in the room.

CHANGE TO A FIVE

Announce that you are able to change a dollar bill into a five. To prove it, roll the bill lengthwise into a tight tube, then bend it to make the numeral 5.

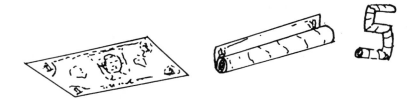

BLOW IT OVER

Fold a crisp bill in half, then bend down two diagonally opposite corners to make it stand on a table like a tiny platform. Challenge your friends to blow it over on its back. After they give up, show them how to do it. Blow the bill across the table until it projects halfway over an edge. Now get down below the table top and blow up on the bill to turn it over.

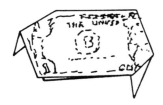

Part 4. COMMON OBJECTS

SUGAR CUBES

CUBE LEVITATION

A tiny dab of butter is secretly stuck to the side of a sugar cube before you show this stunt. Pick up the cube between thumb and finger, the buttered side to the right (figure 1), where it will be invisible from all angles. Another cube is on the tablecloth near a cup of freshly served coffee.

Rub the cube in your hand vigorously against your left jacket sleeve, explaining that this creates a static electrical charge on the sugar. Place the cube on top of the one on the table (figure 2). Press down firmly, then lift the cube as if you were trying to make the lower cube stick to the one in your hand. Nothing happens. Rub it on your sleeve again, and repeat the operation. Again nothing occurs. Look puzzled. Pretend to examine the lower surface of the cube, scraping it a bit with your left thumbnail. All this is intended, of course, to impress the audience with the idea that the cube is unprepared.

Rub the cube on your sleeve for the third time. As you carry it toward the cube on the table, rotate it in the fingers so that the buttered side is down. This time the lower sugar cube sticks to the upper one. Lift the cubes slowly (you can even give them a few shakes) and carry them over to the steaming coffee. Drop them into the cup. You've done a trick, sugared your coffee, and destroyed the evidence!

103

STEADY HANDS

Arrange six sugar cubes as shown. Challenge someone to grasp the two lower cubes between the thumb and forefinger of each hand, lift the entire stack, and drop it into a glass.

You can do it every time, but when the spectator tries it, the stack tumbles over. Present the stunt as a test for "steady nerves."

Secret: When you start to lift the stack, let the tips of your thumbs touch in back. This will steady your hands and make the lift easy.

FIVE-CUBE PICKUP

Here's another amusing "betcha." Arrange five sugar cubes on the table as shown (figure 1) and bet someone he can't pick them all up with one finger. He may curl his finger any way he pleases, but no more than one finger may be used.

Secret: Twist the hand palm up and lift them as shown in figure 2. The thumb is not a "finger"!

1

2

MYSTERIOUS INITIALS

This is an ancient dinner-table classic, but I've included some new angles that add to the presentation. A spectator prints the initial of his last name on a lump of sugar. A soft pencil should be used, and the initials gone over until they are solid and black. While he is doing this, secretly moisten the tip of your right thumb. A good way to do this is to lift your hand to your mouth to conceal a cough.

The sugar is placed on the table, initial side up and with the letter facing you as shown in figure 1. Pick it up between thumb and fingers (figure 2). Carry it to a glass of water and drop it into the water. While the hand is moving toward the glass, the cube is rotated backward so that the moistened thumb presses against the initial. Return the cube immediately to its original position so that when it is dropped into the glass it falls initial side uppermost. Unknown to the audience, you have secured a reverse impression of the initial on your thumb.

Ask the spectator to place his right hand on top of the glass. He will naturally place it palm down. Explain that you prefer to have his hand palm up, and while you say this, reach forward and grasp his hand as shown in figure 3. Turn his hand over so that the back of it rests on the glass. As this is done, the thumb presses against the back of his hand, transferring to it an impression of the initial.

While the sugar is dissolving, call attention to the fact that the carbon particles from the pencil marks are floating to the surface. At the surface, you explain, they release a gas that condenses on the hand. While you talk, you can be wiping your thumb clean with the napkin on your lap.

After the sugar has dissolved, tell him to look at the back of his hand. The initial will appear on the hand as shown in figure 4.

Dorny prefers to say nothing at all about the impression on the hand. After the spectator has removed his hand, he continues his patter about the carbon particles, and while he talks, it slowly occurs to the spectator that maybe there is something on the back of his hand. This makes the final discovery of the impression more dramatic and amusing.

In the hands of Chuck Sanders, Chicago tavern owner and magician, this trick was developed into an unbelievable routine of surprises. The initial appeared not only on the spectator's hand, but also on his wrist and arm, and on the arms of half a dozen other spectators at the bar!

SUGAR PENETRATION

Larry Arcuri of New York City liked to do this one. Unknown to table guests, Larry carefully opened the paper wrapping of a lump of sugar, removed the sugar, then placed the empty paper shell back on the dish. He palmed the sugar in his left hand.

"Most people put sugar in their coffee like this," said Larry. He reached for a piece of sugar, unwrapped it, and dropped it in his coffee, taking care not to expose the palmed piece.

"But a magician does it this way." Larry picked up the empty shell with his right hand, holding his left hand over the coffee, palm down, as shown. The shell rested on top of his hand.

Larry then slapped the shell smartly, at the same time allowing the palmed sugar to fall into the coffee. His right hand then was raised to show the smashed paper wrapper.

HAND TO HAND

Don't let the simplicity of this effect fool you into thinking it isn't deceptive.

Place two sugar cubes near the edge of the table. Pretend to pick them up simultaneously, one in each hand. Actually, the left hand allows its cube to drop into the lap, unnoticed by the audience.

Raise the left hand slowly in the air and *follow it with your eyes*. While attention is concentrated on this hand, the right hand is lowered into the lap, where it picks up the cube. As the left hand is opened to show that the cube has vanished, the right hand is casually raised back into view.

Open the right hand slowly, letting the two cubes roll out.

CUBES, PAPERS, AND COIN

On top of a quarter, stack three sugar cubes. Between the cubes, and projecting to one side as shown, are two small pieces of paper. The challenge is this: Remove the papers and the coin without disturbing the stack or touching it in any way.

Solution: The papers are snapped away with the index finger. Slide a second quarter across the table to knock out the one beneath the stack.

SILVERWARE

BENDING THE SPOON

This joke is not recommended for privately owned silverware, but in a public restaurant with cheap spoons no harm is done. It was a favorite of Henry Gordiene.

Take a spoon between your hands and go through the well-known moves of pretending to bend it, the head of the spoon resting on the table, the handle concealed by your fingers.

Instead of pretending, however, you actually do bend the spoon. A thumb beneath the end of the spoon makes this a simple matter. Bend the spoon until it is almost a right angle.

At this point look up and ask, "How does that look? Does it look as if the spoon is bending?" There will be a chorus of affirmations.

"Well, it should!" you say, as you take the spoon by the handle and hold it up to view.

The spoon can, without damage, be straightened.

SWALLOWING THE KNIFE

This old favorite was described in 1885 in Sachs's *Sleight of Hand,* but here are some new angles.

Place the knife near the edge of the table. Cover it with both hands as shown, and lift it to your mouth, actually taking the knife in your hands. Start to place the blade into your mouth, then change your mind and replace the knife on the table. State that you forgot to *salt* the knife. Take the shaker and sprinkle some salt over it. This is always good for a few chuckles. Pretend to lift the knife once more. This time your hands draw the knife to the edge of the table and permit it to drop into your lap. Keep your hands in the same position as before, as if they still held the knife. Raise them to your mouth, then suddenly pretend to drop the knife down your throat. Show your hands empty and smack your lips.

Someone is sure to ask where the knife went. Lower your hands to your lap and push the knife into your left sleeve. Raise the hands, and extract the knife. The audience will be convinced that the knife went into your sleeve, and will give you credit for some fancy manipulative work.

Another variation is to tip off a friend in advance so that when the audience asks where the knife went, your friend (who is preferably seated at the other end of the table) stands up and shakes a table knife out of *his* sleeve. (You can take advantage of this moment by replacing your knife, unobserved, on the table.)

TABLE KNIFE THROUGH BODY

Hold a cloth napkin by the two upper corners, then swing it over the left arm, as shown in figure 1 on the next page, as if you were about to produce a fishbowl. Exhibit a table knife in the right hand. Appear to place this knife behind the cloth, the point of the knife touching the center of the napkin; and with the knife, lift the cloth from the left arm so that your right hand holds the knife and cloth in the manner shown in figure 2.

Actually, as soon as the knife is behind the napkin, it is pushed into the left sleeve. The right forefinger is extended, and with this finger the napkin is lifted from the arm. The illusion is perfect from the front.

With the left hand, pretend to take the point of the knife through the cloth. The right hand comes out from under the napkin and grasps the cloth at the base. If the left hand pulls on the cloth, it can release its hold and the napkin will retain its shape as if the knife were still inside.

Hold the cloth horizontally (figure 3), then suddenly turn to the person on your left and stab him in the chest with the extended cloth. At the same time your left hand is lowered, permitting the knife to drop into your left palm. With the left hand, reach behind the person's body, under his jacket, and bring out the knife.

This last touch is a product of the nimble brain of Laurie Ireland.

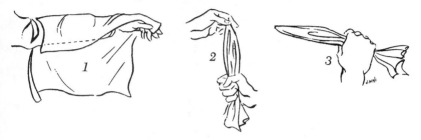

BREAKING THE SPOON

"Everybody knows this old method of *bending* a spoon." As you say this, grasp the spoon and pretend to be bending it, using the familiar method of letting the handle slip through your fists. After having done this, show the spoon to be unharmed, and place it on the edge of the table.

Now look directly into the eyes of the person seated opposite you. This will cause him to look at you. At the same time, pretend to lift the spoon from the table by placing both hands over it. Actually, as soon as your hands cover the spoon, the fingers flip it backward into your lap. Raise your hands as if they held the spoon, keeping your fists next to each other and tightly closed. Lean forward so that your fists are almost under the nose of the person opposite you.

Ask him if he has seen the new method of *breaking* a spoon. When he says no, suddenly pretend to break the spoon in half, making a "pff-fft" noise with your mouth. Immediately open both hands, showing that the spoon has vanished. It never fails to create surprise and astonishment.

I thank Bob Hummer, the vagabond magician, for the misdirection features involved in this sequence of moves.

BALANCING KNIFE AND SPOON

With steady hands, you can balance a knife and spoon on the prongs of a fork as shown. Hold the knife in place until you get the spoon balanced on the tip, then adjust the knife until it balances on the fork. The lower end of the knife handle must rest between the middle prongs of the fork. The spoon and fork are at right angles to each other.

CATCHING THE SALT

Before beginning this trick, shake a small pile of salt on the tablecloth at a spot close to you and to your right. Moisten your right index fingertip with saliva and you're ready to start.

Hold the table knife in the left hand and show both sides to be clean. As you show each side, wipe your thumb across it. On the last wipe, the index finger moistens the lower side of the blade.

Take the knife in the right hand. As your left hand reaches for the salt shaker, the right hand lowers the blade to the tablecloth at the spot where you previously put the salt. Some of the salt will stick to the bottom of the blade.

Meanwhile, the audience is watching the left hand, which shakes some salt from the shaker to the tablecloth. Take a pinch of this salt in the left hand and hold it while the right executes the old paddle move to show both sides of the blade clean. Toss the salt into the air and pretend to catch it on the blade. Of course you merely reverse the blade as you jab the knife forward. Show the salt on the blade. Pretend to wipe off the salt with the palm of the left hand, but under cover of the hand, reverse the blade so that the left palm slides over the clean side. Show both sides clean by the paddle move. Place a pinch of salt on the blade, toss it into the air, and catch it a second time. Clean the blade with a napkin. This routine was worked out by Walter Price.

CROSS OF KNIVES

Two table knives can be crossed and held by the finger and thumb as indicated. It takes a little practice to acquire the knack of getting them in place, but once you've mastered it you have an interesting "betcha." Few people are able to duplicate the feat, even if you let them inspect the position of your fingers carefully.

DIVER IN THE SPOON

I'm indebted to Abril Lamarque, of New York City, for this one. Hold the spoon in the left hand, as shown in figure 1 on the next page. The polished back serves as a mirror. If the right hand is held as pictured, the reflection in the spoon will resemble the back of a man about to dive from the edge of the table. The first and fourth fingers are his arms, extended backward in readiness for the dive. Move these fingers up and down. In the spoon it will look as if he is swinging his arms back and forth, getting ready to jump. On the last downward swing of the fingers, lift the hand backward into the air, describing an arc indicated by the arrow in figure 2. In the reflection it looks as if the man dived off the edge of a pool.

Bert Easely uses the dive as a climax for his "woman in the tub" routine. The spoon is held as shown in figure 3, the spoon resting on the second and third fingers, just below the knuckles. By keeping the first and second fingers bent and moving them up and down slightly, you get an image resembling a woman in a tub, her back to you, scrubbing herself.

Bert's routine begins with the woman taking the soap from the soap dish (done by extending the little finger to the right). She then scrubs herself, drops the soap, bends forward to pick it up, washes her left foot (done by tilting the hand to the right and wiggling the index finger), then her right foot (tilt the hand to the left and wiggle the little finger), puts back the soap, and finally dives out of the tub!

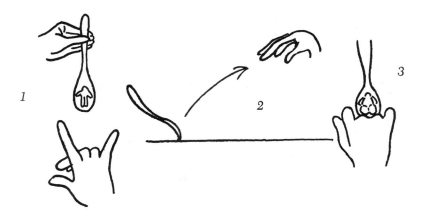

THE MUSICAL KNIFE

This is an old stunt, but one of the most entertaining when properly presented. Hold a fork in the left hand so that the handle is almost touching the table. Take a table knife in the right hand and, with the blade, pluck one of the center prongs of the fork. Immediately hold the tip of the knife blade over an empty tumbler. At the instant the knife is above the glass, the left hand allows the handle of the fork to rest on the table. This will produce a musical note, easily heard unless you are in a very noisy restaurant. Do this several times, stating that the note occurs only when the knife is held over something *empty*. Place two empty glasses side by side and move the blade of the knife from one to the other. The left hand raises and lowers the handle of the fork so that the tone occurs only when the knife is directly over the brim of each glass.

Conclude the effect by holding the blade over the *head* of the person nearest to you!

I am indebted to Dorny for this routine and finish.

SPOON TO KNIFE

The effect is as follows. A spoon is wrapped in a cloth napkin. When the napkin is unrolled, the spoon has changed into a table knife.

Spread the napkin on the table as shown in figure 1, with the knife concealed beneath it. Place the spoon on the cloth just *behind* the knife. Now fold the corner nearest you over to meet the opposite corner. Note that the corner on top must be an inch or so *behind* the lower corner.

Start to roll the spoon in the napkin, making the roll *beneath* the napkin so that the knife is included in the roll. After rolling forward a few inches, turn the napkin over, bring the roll upward, and continue rolling forward until you reach the far corners. As you complete the roll, one end of the cloth is permitted to go around the roll once, so that it comes flush with the other corner. This is concealed by the hands, which are held over the center of the roll as it is rolled forward on the table.

Place the fingers of the left hand on the *lower* corner, holding it against the table. The right hand takes the *upper* corner and pulls it toward you, unrolling the napkin. This automatically causes the spoon to drop into your lap (this is concealed by the cloth) and exposes the knife inside the napkin!

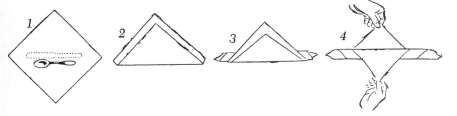

GLASSES

I.Q. TEST

Place a cardboard menu over a glass of water, invert it, put it on the table, then pull out the menu. This leaves the glass upside down, the water still inside. The problem is how to get the glass right side up again without getting water all over the table.

Solution: Slide the glass to the edge of the table so that a portion of the rim projects, and let the water drain into another glass.

BRIM TO BRIM

Two glasses, each filled with water, are placed brim to brim as shown. They rest in a small dessert dish. Two unusual puzzles can be presented.

1. Can you place a dime inside the glasses without spilling any water?

Solution: Look carefully around the rims until you find a spot where the rims are not quite touching. If you can't find such a spot, tap the lower glass lightly with the dime until an opening shows up. The coin can be pushed through this opening without spilling any water.

2. Can you remove the water from the upper glass without touching the glasses in any way?

Solution: Blow through a soda straw at the spot where you inserted the dime. The end of the straw does not touch the rims. Air will bubble up through the upper glass forcing the water out through the rims and into the dish below.

Perhaps you are wondering how to get the two glasses brim to brim in the first place. That's easy. Plunge them below the surface of the water in a kitchen sink, put the brims together, and lift them out!

Note: At a restaurant table you can use two creamers instead of glasses. Fill them both with water, hold a business card over one of them, turn it upside down atop the other creamer, pull out the card, and you're all set.

PROBLEM OF THE SIX GLASSES

Arrange six glasses in a row, as shown on the next page. The three on the right are filled with water. The other three are empty. The problem is to arrange the glasses so that they alternate, full and empty. You are allowed to move only one glass.

Solution: Pick up glass number five, pour its contents into glass number two, then replace it in its original position.

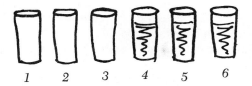

THE PYRAMID

This is an easy bit of table jugglery, but it looks dangerous.

Form a pyramid with six glasses as shown. The pyramid rests on the edge of a cloth napkin. A second napkin is between the first and second level of glasses, and a third napkin is between the second level and the single glass on top. The pyramid should be near the edge of the table, and the napkins must have at least one side without a hem. The hemless edges are indicated in the illustration.

Note also that each glass is half-filled with water. This makes the trick look harder, but actually gives the glasses greater stability.

Grasp the free, hanging edge of the upper napkin and give it a quick horizontal yank. It will pull out easily without disturbing the glasses. Repeat with the middle napkin, and lastly, with the bottom one.

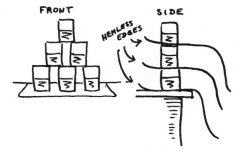

PENNY GAME

Wet the brim of a glass and place a paper napkin on top. Tear away the napkin so that it leaves a circle of paper covering the opening of the glass. Place a penny in the center of the paper.

Two people, each holding a burning cigarette, play the game. The first player touches his cigarette to the napkin just long enough to produce a small hole. The second player does likewise. This continues by turns until one of the players loses by causing the penny to drop into the glass. Elaborate filigree will be produced before the penny finally falls.

After a game has been played, use a piece of flash paper for the second game. The other player, of course, goes first!

NAPKINS AND HANDKERCHIEFS

PHANTOM NAPKIN

Place a cloth napkin over your left fist. Extend the hand and ask a spectator to push the center of the cloth into the fist. After he does so, remark that the well isn't quite deep enough.

Insert your index finger (as shown in figure 1 on the next page) to push it deeper. The middle finger extends downward, on the right side of the cloth, so that it rests in the crotch formed by the fingers of the left fist and the tip of the left thumb. Open the fist slightly and grab the middle finger through the cloth (figure 2). The first and second fingers are now inside the well. Remove the index finger and rotate the hand to the right and left several times to strengthen the sides of the well (figure 3). This shift of fingers will produce an invisible tube of cloth extending all the way through the napkin.

An even simpler way to form the tube is as follows: When your left hand comes back, after the spectator has formed the well, bring your middle finger into the well by extending it downward and moving it into the fist from the side, exactly as described above. In other words, the middle finger goes immediately into the fist, carrying the side of the napkin with it. If you hold the left hand to the right side of your body, the move will take place in the rear. No one will notice that the finger enters the well from the side and not from above.

Insert a table knife into the well. Tip the fist to let everyone see that the well is really in the center of the cloth. Allow the knife to fall through to the table, or reach underneath, take the handle, and move the knife up and down a few times, finally withdrawing it from below. Apparently the knife has penetrated the cloth.

Hold the left hand on the right side of the body, tilting the opening toward the audience. The right hand reaches down behind the fist and finds the upper edge of the napkin. This is the edge that was pushed into the fist. The left fingers open slightly, allowing this edge to pop out of the fist where it has been compressed. Raise the edge upward to the position shown in figure 4.

The left fist is still grasping the original well. The right hand continues to pull upward on the cloth until the well is pulled out of the fist. Do this slowly, calling attention to the fact that the well actually is in the center of the napkin.

This last bit of business looks very convincing.

Seymour Davis, of Stillwater, Oklahoma, is the inventor of this fine trick. It sold on the market many years ago under the name of "Seymour's Phantom Hanky."

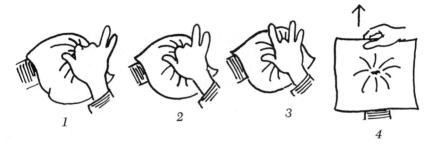

SAUCY OLD WOMAN

Break a cigarette in half and clip the pieces between the second and third fingers (as in figure 1 on the next page). Wrap a table napkin around the hand (figure 2) to form the old woman's hood. The top of the hood is held in place by clipping the cloth between the third and little fingers. The right hand pinches together the cloth beneath the chin as indicated.

The likeness to a toothless old woman is startling! The knuckle of your middle finger makes the nose, the cigarettes form the eyes, and the mouth is produced by the opening between the first and second fingers. To make the woman talk, wiggle the index finger up and down. If you do ventriloquist work, you can ask her questions.

For a final guffaw, have the old woman stick out her tongue at one of the table guests. This is done by pushing the thumb out between the first and second fingers.

STRETCHING THE NAPKIN

In the older method of stretching a napkin or handkerchief, it was necessary to get the ends wadded up in the hands. For close-up work, this is hard to conceal. A newer and cleaner method is as follows:

Fold the napkin as shown. Take the upper corners in each hand, the thumb and index finger of each hand clipping the corners nearest you, and the index and middle finger clipping the other corners. Whirl the cloth to form it into a rope. Release the front corner from one hand and the back corner from the other. Continue whirling and pulling after each whirl. The cloth will stretch to its full diagonal length, almost twice the original.

LEMON BUG

Twist the four corners of a paper napkin as shown in the drawing on the next page. Secretly place a lemon underneath. If you punch the "bug" with your finger, it will zigzag over the table in a very curious and erratic fashion, as if alive. Keep shoving it about awhile to build up curiosity as to what devilish device is beneath, then let someone lift the napkin. The disclosure of a mere lemon will draw plenty of added laughs. You can add eyes to the bug, as shown, by using a felt-tip pen.

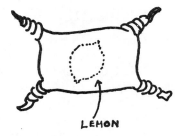

LEMON

CHARACTER READING FROM THE TEETH

Tell your table companions that you have recently learned the art of reading character from the biting impressions of a person's teeth. To prove it, pass a cloth napkin around the table, asking each person to bite into the cloth to leave an impression. Take back the napkin and study the impressions carefully. Then put it down, saying, "You folks certainly bit on that one."

IMPROVISED BRASSIERE

I have been unable to discover the source of this clever napkin stunt. The napkin is placed flat on the table as in figure 1. The right and left sides are folded to the center as in figure 2. Grasp the napkin in each hand at points X and Y, lifting it so that it folds backward along line XY. Lay it on the table again in the position shown in figure 3. Take the two corners on the left between the thumb and fingers of the left hand, and the two on the right in the right hand. Bring the hands suddenly against the chest, as in figure 4, with surprising results. There are so many patter versions that might accompany this stunt, I have left them to the reader's imagination.

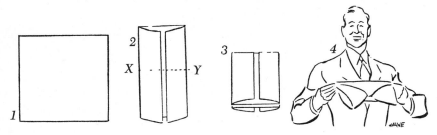

HANDKERCHIEF ESCAPE

Ask a spectator to extend the index finger of his right hand. Hold a handkerchief by opposite corners and swing it in circles, skip-rope fashion, until it twists into a cloth rope. Place this rolled-up handkerchief over the extended finger as shown in figure 1. Now follow these directions carefully:

1. Cross the handkerchief underneath (figure 2). Note that the end marked "A" is toward you at the crossing point. Throughout the rest of the moves this same end must always be toward you when the ends cross. Otherwise the trick won't work.

2. Cross the ends above (figure 3).

3. Have the spectator place the index finger of his left hand on top of the crossing (figure 4).

4. Cross the ends above his left finger, taking care to keep the proper end toward you (figure 5).

5. Cross the ends beneath (figure 6).

6. Bring the ends up and hold them in the left hand (figure 7). The two fingers are now securely wrapped together.

7. Take hold of the tip of the lower finger. Ask him to remove his upper finger from the cloth. As soon as he does so, lift up with your left hand. The handkerchief will pull free of the finger you are holding (figure 8).

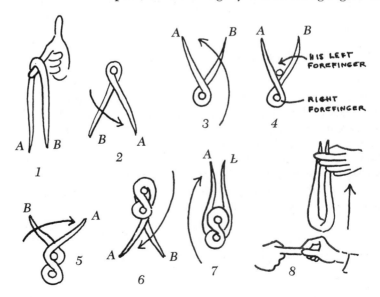

THE INVISIBLE HAIR

You must have a cloth napkin, well starched, for this amusing stunt. Take the center of the cloth in the right hand and draw it up through the left fist. The napkin will retain its shape so that the hand can hold it as shown in the first drawing. With the right hand, pretend to pluck a hair from the head of the nearest person, and tie one end of it around the tip of the napkin. Hold your right hand about a foot to the right, as if it held the free end of the hair. Move your right hand back and forth. At the same time, the thumb of the left hand moves up and down. This causes the napkin to bend over to the right and back up again. With a little practice you can harmonize the motions of the napkin and the hand so that they give a perfect illusion of a hair attached to the tip of the cloth.

As a finish, pull the cloth over as far as you can to the right, then bend over and pretend to *bite* the hair in two. As you click your teeth together, the left thumb allows the cloth to spring upright.

RING VANISH

Borrow a ring and hold it in the left fingers. Cover the hand with a cloth napkin. The right hand grasps the front edge of the cloth and raises it to give the audience a last look at the ring. As the hand returns the edge to its former position, the left hand drops the ring so that it falls into the right fingers.

Raise the left hand, looking at it and pattering about the ring, while the right hand goes into your lap and slips the ring on a finger.

The right hand now takes an edge of the napkin and pulls it slowly from the left hand. The ring is gone. Call attention to the ring on your finger, remove it, and return it to the owner.

THE VANISHING SALT SHAKER

This is one of the most startling table tricks. Its success depends almost wholly on the use of misdirection.

Place a coin (say, a dime) on the table before you. On the coin, place a salt shaker. Cover the shaker with a cloth napkin (folded twice), pressing the cloth around the shaker so that it assumes the shape of the shaker. If paper napkins are available, so much the better. Use three or four of them together.

State that you intend to cause the dime to vanish. Make some passes over the shaker, mumble some double-talk, then lift the shaker and napkin, drawing them back toward the edge of the table. As you do this, lean forward and push the dime forward with a finger of your free hand. All eyes will be misdirected toward the coin. This permits you to let the shaker drop into your lap. The napkin retains the shape of the shaker. Shake your head as if the trick had failed and cover the dime once more. Repeat the passes and the double-talk. Remove the napkin, but the dime is still there. This is buildup to strengthen the belief of the audience that the shaker is still beneath the cloth.

Pretend to be thinking, then say, "No wonder the trick isn't working. It's not the dime that's supposed to vanish, but the salt shaker." As you say this, smash the napkin to the table with your fist.

As a variation, start the trick with a *pepper* shaker on your lap. State that you intend to cause the dime to change into a penny. When you drop the salt shaker, your left hand comes up and pushes the pepper shaker into the napkin. After the trick has apparently failed, state that you had it all wrong. It's the salt shaker that changes, not the coin. Take away the napkin and show this to be the case.

PULL-APART NAPKINS

Twist two cloth napkins rope fashion and cross one over the other, holding them in the left hand, as shown in figure 1. With the right hand, reach under and take end "A," wrapping it once around the other napkin (figure 2).

Now grasp end "B" of the second napkin, and carry it under and around the first one as indicated (figure 3). In both cases the ends must go *under* the other napkin, then up and across. Bring ends "B" and "C" together *below* in the right hand, and ends "A" and "D" together *above* in the left (figure 4). Apparently you have wrapped each napkin once around the other. Yet when you give them a yank, they pull apart!

If the illustrations are followed carefully, the trick will work itself. With silks, you can wrap each cloth *twice* around the other. They still come apart!

Edwin Tabor, of Berkeley, California, invented this unusual trick.

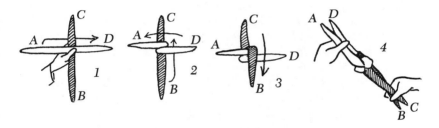

MISCELLANEOUS

CRAZY CRACKERS

This beautiful little table illusion is the invention of Val Evans. It's included here with the kind permission of Lloyd Jones, who marketed it under the name of Optogramma.

A good way to begin is to pick up a soda cracker, of the square variety, and hold it between the thumb and middle finger (as shown in figure 1 on the next page). Blow on the corner indicated. If the cracker is not held tightly, it will spin rapidly in the fingers. Explain that you are testing the cracker to make sure it rotates properly.

Place the cracker on the tablecloth. With a pencil or borrowed lipstick, draw a vertical line as shown in figure 2. Lift the cracker a few inches above the table, holding it by corners "A" and "B." Place the tip of the left index finger on corner "X" and rotate the cracker once. Replace it on the table. Draw another vertical line.

Pick up the cracker, holding it the same way (figure 3), and with the left forefinger at corner "X," rotate it from side to side rapidly. The line will appear to run the same way on both sides. Remark that the marks run "north and south" on each side. Give the cracker a quarter-turn to the left so that the mark is horizontal (figure 4). Hold it by the corners and rotate it again, explaining that if the cracker is held in this position, the two lines run "east and west." Reach under the cracker and pretend you are twisting the underneath line so it will be at right angles to the other.

Put the cracker on the table, with the line vertical. With the tip of the index finger, lift up the edge nearest you and flip the cracker forward so that it turns over on its back. The line showing will be horizontal! Flip the cracker forward several times, causing it to somersault its way across the tablecloth so that everyone can see that the two lines are at right angles. Crumble it up before anyone has a chance to experiment with it.

With two soda crackers, a transposition effect can be obtained. On the first cracker, draw the lines in the manner described. That is, they appear to be the same on both sides, but are actually at right angles. On the second cracker, draw the first line vertically, then rotate it in the manner previously described, and draw the second line horizontally.

Place the crackers in front of you. Pick up the first and rotate it several times to show that the line is north and south on both sides. Replace it on the table. In front of it place a single match (figure 5).

Pick up the second cracker, rotating it to show that the lines are at right angles. Place it beside the first, marking it with two crossed matches (figure 5).

Pick up a cracker in each hand, cross the arms, and replace them. You have switched the positions of the crackers. But when you somersault them forward, each cracker corresponds to the match markers as before!

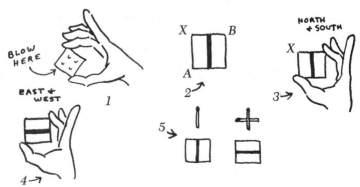

SCHOKE'S WISE CRACKER

Remember the old stunt of marking one side of a paper match and offering to bet a beer that when the match is dropped it will alight on its edge rather than on either side? The secret was to bend the match before you dropped it. Chic Schoke, of Chicago's Round Table, liked to do it with a soda cracker.

"If the cracker falls with the smooth side up," Chic would say, "I'll buy you a beer. If it lights rough side up, I'll buy you two beers. But if it falls in some way so that neither side is up [at this point Chic held the cracker on its edge] then you'll owe me a beer. Fair enough?" At that point Chic would raise his hand, crumble the cracker in his fist, and toss the crumbs over everybody present!

THUMB-TIP QUICKIE

Remember the old schoolboy stunt of trying to catch your thumb? The thumb is pushed up through the left fist, then the right hand withdraws and makes a quick sweeping motion over the top of the fist as if trying to catch the thumb. In his book *A Conjuring Melange,* Stanley Collins has an amusing switch on this.

With a thumb tip on the right thumb, go through the motions just described, keeping the right thumb concealed behind the fingers as you make the "catch" motion. Explain that catching the thumb is difficult unless you "sneak up" on it. As you say this, withdraw the right hand slowly, leaving the thumb tip projecting from the fist. Still in slow motion, the right hand picks up the tip and places it in the pocket.

THE SAILOR AND THE DOUGHNUT

"A man entered a restaurant and ordered two cups of coffee." As you say this, place a cup and saucer on your left and another cup and saucer on your right.

"He then ordered a single doughnut, which he broke in half, placing one half on the left saucer and one on the right." Illustrate with a doughnut, if one is handy; otherwise pretend to do it, with an imaginary doughnut.

"The waitress watched this operation and said, 'I see you're a sailor.'"
How did she know he was a sailor?
After everyone gives up, reveal the answer: He had on a sailor suit!

UP THE SCALE

Everyone knows that you can pinch the end of a paper soda straw, then blow through it to make a noise like a foghorn. Not everyone knows that if you cut off the end of the straw, it will raise the pitch of the tone. Here's an amusing way to make use of this fact.

First make the horn. While you're blowing it, take a pair of scissors from your pocket and start chopping off the end. Keep blowing and keep chopping until you reach your mouth. The result will be a series of tones from the low-pitched note at the beginning to a high, piercing note at the finish. With a little practice you can run a pretty good scale.

FINANCIAL SPECTACLES

This calls for a little preparation. Buy a cheap pair of glasses at the dime store and paste a black dollar mark on each lens. You can cut the dollar marks out of black paper, or the black portion of a magazine picture. Carry the glasses in your pocket.

The next time you get into a conversation involving money, such as a discussion of who pays the dinner check, say, "Excuse me a moment while I put on my financial glasses." Whip out the prepared specs, put them on, lean forward, and ask, "Now, what were you saying?"

MENTAL PREDICTION

On the back of a piece of paper (without letting the audience see what you're writing) put the word "blue," the figure of a triangle, and the number 37. Place the sheet in front of someone, blank side up. Ask him to write the name of a color. Explain that nine out of ten people write "red," so you would prefer he *not* use this color. Almost invariably he will choose blue.

Under the color, request that he draw "some simple geometric figure, such as a square or circle." Since you mention these two figures, he'll probably eliminate them and draw a triangle.

Finally, ask him to write a two-figure number between 1 and 50, both figures of which are odd. Specify further that the same numeral must not be repeated, such as 1 and 1. For some curious reason, 37 is almost always chosen.

Turn over the paper to show your predictions. If you miss one or more of the items, you can pass it off as a psychological test that doesn't always work. But you'll be astounded how many times you hit all three correctly.

MORE PREDICTION

Write a prediction and place it aside, face down. Ask someone to write down the following words:

1. The name of a nation that begins with the letter *D*.
2. The name of an animal that begins with the second letter of that nation's name.
3. The color of that animal.
4. The name of an animal that begins with the last letter of that nation's name.
5. The name of a fruit that begins with the last letter of the second animal's name.

Your prediction, almost always accurate on all counts, is: Denmark, elephant, gray, kangaroo, orange.

THE FIFTY SPONGE BALLS

Matt Schulien, Chicago's famous card magician and close-up worker, has generously allowed me to give here his climax for the comeback sponge trick. Cut about fifty small sponge balls, about an inch in diameter, from a rubber bath sponge. Carry them in the right side pocket of your jacket. Place three small sponges on the table, keeping a fourth concealed in the right hand. A good way to palm it is the manner perfected by Audley Walsh—clipped between the second and third fingers, which are curled back out of sight.

Ask someone to point to one of the sponges on the table. Pick it up between the thumb and index finger, placing it in the left hand. Have a second sponge designated. This time, as the thumb and finger take the sponge, the second and third fingers are extended and the two sponges are squeezed together as one. Open the left hand and openly place the second sponge (really two sponges) into the hand.

The right hand now picks up the remaining sponge and pretends to place it in the right jacket pocket. Actually, the hand comes out of the pocket with the sponge palmed as before. Open the left hand to show the three sponges.

Repeat this several times. Now for the surprising climax: The last time the right hand goes to the pocket, it grabs a handful of sponge balls. Grab as many as you can. You'll be astonished at the number that can be compressed into the fist.

To cover up the fact that the right hand is closed into a fist, time its removal from the pocket so it occurs at the same instant that you open your left hand to roll the three balls to the table. Better yet, work the last "comeback" in the spectator's hand. This will direct attention to his hand and no one will notice that your right hand is formed into a fist. As soon as the three sponges are revealed, pick up one with the *left* hand and push it into the right fist, explaining, "This time we'll try the same trick using the *other* hand." Push the second ball into the fist. Pick up the third and place it in your *left* jacket pocket.

At this point pause and ask how many sponges are in your right hand. Many will say "Three," and if you're lucky, someone may suspect a new twist and yell "None!"

Open your right hand and roll out the dozens of little sponges!

I know of no table trick that provides a more unexpected climax.

SWIZZLE-STICK STUNTS

The fact that a glass stirring rod, held over print, will cause the letters to turn upside down makes possible many amusing word stunts. The two stunts below require only a sheet of paper and a pencil.

1. Print the phrase "Choice Bock—50¢," forming the letters and numerals exactly as shown. Explain that this used to be the price for a bottle of bock beer. To find out how much the bottle cost before inflation, read the sentence through the rod. The price is "deflated" to 20¢, but the rest of the phrase remains unchanged!

2. Print the sentence "bob kicked pop," forming the letters as indicated. To find out what happened after this event occurred, read it through the swizzle stick. The sentence changes to "pop kicked bob."

CHOICE BOCK — 50¢

bob KICKED pop

KNUCKLE POPPING

Obtain a metal "snapper" of the type usually available in the toy section of a dime store or at novelty counters. Palm it in the right hand. The third and fourth fingers curl back so that they can operate the snapper.

At the opportune moment, say to your companions, "I hope no one will be annoyed if I pop my knuckles. I do this after every meal." As you say this, take hold of each finger of the left hand and bend it upward. As you bend the finger, the right third finger presses the snapper. When you release the finger, allow the metal strip to snap back again.

It sounds exactly as if you are cracking your knuckles, except the noise is about ten times louder. The bigger the snapper, the louder the noise.

TRAVELING FOUNTAIN PEN

A borrowed fountain pen (or automatic pencil) is caused to travel invisibly from your inner jacket pocket to that of the man on your right. He is tipped off in advance.

Borrow a fountain pen. Take it in the left hand and appear to place it in the inside jacket pocket, saying "That's a fine-looking pen, mind if I keep it?" Actually, drop it down the right jacket sleeve, near the armpit. The right arm hangs normally at the side, so the pen drops noiselessly into the fingers.

Remove the left hand from the jacket, open the fingers wide, and look at the hand. While the attention of the audience is on this hand, the right hand drops the pen into the lap of the person on the right, who quietly clips it to his jacket pocket while everyone is watching you.

By this time the owner of the pen is asking to have it returned. "But," you protest, "I really haven't got the pen. However, I believe the gentleman on my right can return it to you." If your stooge is a convincing actor, the trick can be built into a real piece of magic.

In the absence of a stooge, slip the pen under a napkin on the table, and produce it later by removing the napkin to expose it.

VANISHING COFFEE STEAM

The magician waves his hand over his coffee and the steam suddenly stops rising from the cup!

Secret: Either the magician or a confederate seated next to him blows gently at the cup. Waving the hands misdirects attention from your lips, which should appear as normal as possible.

STIRRING-STICK MOVIES

Wooden stirring sticks shaped like the one in figure 1 on the next page are widely used in bars and restaurants where mixed drinks are served. Here's an amusing stunt with one of them.

With a pencil, draw the two figures shown in figure 2, one on each side of the stick. This should be done before you show the trick.

Hold the stick in your right hand and show the picture of the man standing up. Make the old paddle move to show him standing on both sides. Wave the stick in the air, secretly reversing it. The man is now in a crouching position. Repeat the paddle move to show him in this position on both sides.

Then hold the stick as shown in figure 3. By sliding the thumb and finger back and forth you cause the stick to flip rapidly from one picture to the other. The result is a lifelike moving picture of a man doing his morning setting-up exercises.

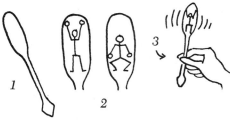

CATCHING THE CHECK

A restaurant check can be used for an amusing bit of byplay. Hold it as shown. Ask someone at the table to keep his hand in position to grab the check, but with his fingers and thumb not quite touching it. Tell him you are going to drop the check. Ask him to try to catch it between his thumb and fingers. If he can catch it once in three tries, you'll pay the bill.

It looks easy, but actually the check is impossible to grab. It takes too long for the visual impression to reach the brain and send the signal to the fingers.

To make it more exasperating, demonstrate how easy it is by holding the check in one hand and catching it with the other. You can do it yourself because your brain knows when you let go. A dollar bill, of course, will work as well as a check.

TAPPING TABLE OBJECTS

I first ran across a version of this table effect in Walter B. Gibson's *New Magician's Manual.*

The magician arranges seven objects in front of him on the table. A spectator is asked to think of one of the seven. The magician starts tapping the objects with his table knife. At each tap the spectator is to spell (to himself) a letter in the name of the object he has in mind. When he completes the spelling, he says "Stop." This is done. When he says "Stop" he discovers, to his surprise, that the magician is touching the chosen object with his knife.

The seven objects used are as follows: 1. cup; 2. fork; 3. plate; 4. napkin; 5. ashtray; 6. matchbox; 7. cigarette.

This list must be memorized. In presenting the trick it is necessary to make the first two taps on any objects you wish, then start tapping them in the order indicated by the list.

The trick is puzzling enough to withstand several repetitions.

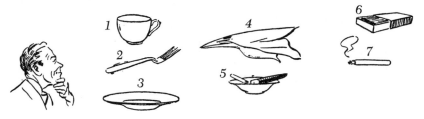

BETWEEN THE TEETH

Prepare a toothpick by fastening a dozen or more small strands of colored thread to the end as illustrated. Use thick thread. The wide end of the pick can be notched, and the strands secured by wrapping a thread tightly around the end and tying it. Carry the pick in your pocket.

After a meal, take out the pick, with the colored threads wrapped around the end and concealed in the hand. Raise the pick to your mouth. Under cover of the hand, lever the prepared end into your mouth.

Pretend to pick your teeth, making wild facial grimaces as you probe about. Remove the pick, with the colored threads dangling.

"You never know what you'll find between your teeth," you can say.

FLAPPING PAPER

There are three reasons why I feel justified in including this item in the book.

One: it is the most ingenious and entertaining paper-folded toy ever invented.

Two: Very few people, including magicians, have seen it.

Three: It lends itself to one or two novel presentations.

Rather than repeat here the complex instructions necessary in order to explain how the bird is folded, let me refer the reader to Houdini's *Paper Magic*, page 117, where the method of folding is described. The earliest description I have found of this item is in Tissandier's *Scientific Recreations*, a French work published in 1881 and later translated into English. (You will also find the folding described in Chapter 16 of my *Second Scientific American Book of Mathematical Puzzles and Diversions*.)

The bird itself is extremely lifelike. When the tail is pulled, it flaps its wings. It can be folded from any type of paper, and from a square of almost any size. It never fails to delight persons of all ages.

Carry some four-inch squares of flash paper with you. Fold the bird from one of them. Pass it around the table so that others can have the fun of operating it, then place it on top of an inverted glass. Patter about the bird's extreme fear of fire. To illustrate why, touch a lit cigarette to the bird's tail.

Another presentation angle is to conceal a dime in your hand, dropping it into the paper (in this case a larger piece of ordinary paper) while you are folding it, so that the dime will later be inside the bird's body. Refer to the bird as a "magpie" and patter about its love of coins. Often it swallows the money that it carries in its bill, you say. Tear open the body and shake out the dime.

Or better, have a borrowed dime marked, and fold it in a piece of paper, making the usual fold so that the dime drops into the hand. Then fold the bird from another sheet of paper, leaving the dime inside. Fly the bird over to the folded paper, touching its bill to the place where the dime is supposed to be. Then tear up the paper to prove that the dime has vanished, and find the coin inside the body of the bird.

PENETRATING RUBBER BAND

Extend your index finger and ask someone to hold its tip firmly while you hang a rubber band over the same hand's little finger. Tell him to close his eyes. When he opens them, the band is hanging from your index finger!

Secret: A duplicate band is around your wrist, concealed under the sleeve. Simply remove the band from your little finger and pocket it. Then slide the other band off your wrist, over your hand, and onto your index finger, where it hangs.

To conceal the method from others who may be watching, you can drape a handkerchief over your hand. Beneath it, slide the band from your wrist, then carry the other band away with the handkerchief as you remove it and put it in your pocket.

I found this charming trick in Richard Kaufman's book *Five Times Five*, where it is described by Japanese magician Ken Kuroki.

A CATALOG OF SELECTED
DOVER BOOKS
IN ALL FIELDS OF INTEREST

A CATALOG OF SELECTED DOVER
BOOKS IN ALL FIELDS OF INTEREST

CONCERNING THE SPIRITUAL IN ART, Wassily Kandinsky. Pioneering work by father of abstract art. Thoughts on color theory, nature of art. Analysis of earlier masters. 12 illustrations. 80pp. of text. 5⅜ x 8½. 23411-8 Pa. $4.95

ANIMALS: 1,419 Copyright-Free Illustrations of Mammals, Birds, Fish, Insects, etc., Jim Harter (ed.). Clear wood engravings present, in extremely lifelike poses, over 1,000 species of animals. One of the most extensive pictorial sourcebooks of its kind. Captions. Index. 284pp. 9 x 12. 23766-4 Pa. $14.95

CELTIC ART: The Methods of Construction, George Bain. Simple geometric techniques for making Celtic interlacements, spirals, Kells-type initials, animals, humans, etc. Over 500 illustrations. 160pp. 9 x 12. (USO) 22923-8 Pa. $9.95

AN ATLAS OF ANATOMY FOR ARTISTS, Fritz Schider. Most thorough reference work on art anatomy in the world. Hundreds of illustrations, including selections from works by Vesalius, Leonardo, Goya, Ingres, Michelangelo, others. 593 illustrations. 192pp. 7⅛ x 10¼. 20241-0 Pa. $9.95

CELTIC HAND STROKE-BY-STROKE (Irish Half-Uncial from "The Book of Kells"): An Arthur Baker Calligraphy Manual, Arthur Baker. Complete guide to creating each letter of the alphabet in distinctive Celtic manner. Covers hand position, strokes, pens, inks, paper, more. Illustrated. 48pp. 8¼ x 11. 24336-2 Pa. $3.95

EASY ORIGAMI, John Montroll. Charming collection of 32 projects (hat, cup, pelican, piano, swan, many more) specially designed for the novice origami hobbyist. Clearly illustrated easy-to-follow instructions insure that even beginning papercrafters will achieve successful results. 48pp. 8¼ x 11. 27298-2 Pa. $3.50

THE COMPLETE BOOK OF BIRDHOUSE CONSTRUCTION FOR WOODWORKERS, Scott D. Campbell. Detailed instructions, illustrations, tables. Also data on bird habitat and instinct patterns. Bibliography. 3 tables. 63 illustrations in 15 figures. 48pp. 5¼ x 8½. 24407-5 Pa. $2.50

BLOOMINGDALE'S ILLUSTRATED 1886 CATALOG: Fashions, Dry Goods and Housewares, Bloomingdale Brothers. Famed merchants' extremely rare catalog depicting about 1,700 products: clothing, housewares, firearms, dry goods, jewelry, more. Invaluable for dating, identifying vintage items. Also, copyright-free graphics for artists, designers. Co-published with Henry Ford Museum & Greenfield Village. 160pp. 8¼ x 11. 25780-0 Pa. $10.95

HISTORIC COSTUME IN PICTURES, Braun & Schneider. Over 1,450 costumed figures in clearly detailed engravings–from dawn of civilization to end of 19th century. Captions. Many folk costumes. 256pp. 8⅜ x 11¾. 23150-X Pa. $12.95

THE INFLUENCE OF SEA POWER UPON HISTORY, 1660–1783, A. T. Mahan. Influential classic of naval history and tactics still used as text in war colleges. First paperback edition. 4 maps. 24 battle plans. 640pp. 5⅜ x 8½. 25509-3 Pa. $14.95

THE STORY OF THE TITANIC AS TOLD BY ITS SURVIVORS, Jack Winocour (ed.). What it was really like. Panic, despair, shocking inefficiency, and a little heroism. More thrilling than any fictional account. 26 illustrations. 320pp. 5⅜ x 8½. 20610-6 Pa. $8.95

FAIRY AND FOLK TALES OF THE IRISH PEASANTRY, William Butler Yeats (ed.). Treasury of 64 tales from the twilight world of Celtic myth and legend: "The Soul Cages," "The Kildare Pooka," "King O'Toole and his Goose," many more. Introduction and Notes by W. B. Yeats. 352pp. 5⅜ x 8½. 26941-8 Pa. $8.95

BUDDHIST MAHAYANA TEXTS, E. B. Cowell and Others (eds.). Superb, accurate translations of basic documents in Mahayana Buddhism, highly important in history of religions. The Buddha-karita of Asvaghosha, Larger Sukhavativyuha, more. 448pp. 5⅜ x 8½. 25552-2 Pa. $12.95

ONE TWO THREE . . . INFINITY: Facts and Speculations of Science, George Gamow. Great physicist's fascinating, readable overview of contemporary science: number theory, relativity, fourth dimension, entropy, genes, atomic structure, much more. 128 illustrations. Index. 352pp. 5⅜ x 8½. 25664-2 Pa. $8.95

ENGINEERING IN HISTORY, Richard Shelton Kirby, et al. Broad, nontechnical survey of history's major technological advances: birth of Greek science, industrial revolution, electricity and applied science, 20th-century automation, much more. 181 illustrations. ". . . excellent . . ."–*Isis*. Bibliography. vii + 530pp. 5⅜ x 8¼. 26412-2 Pa. $14.95

DALÍ ON MODERN ART: The Cuckolds of Antiquated Modern Art, Salvador Dalí. Influential painter skewers modern art and its practitioners. Outrageous evaluations of Picasso, Cézanne, Turner, more. 15 renderings of paintings discussed. 44 calligraphic decorations by Dalí. 96pp. 5⅜ x 8½. (USO) 29220-7 Pa. $4.95

ANTIQUE PLAYING CARDS: A Pictorial History, Henry René D'Allemagne. Over 900 elaborate, decorative images from rare playing cards (14th–20th centuries): Bacchus, death, dancing dogs, hunting scenes, royal coats of arms, players cheating, much more. 96pp. 9¼ x 12¼. 29265-7 Pa. $12.95

MAKING FURNITURE MASTERPIECES: 30 Projects with Measured Drawings, Franklin H. Gottshall. Step-by-step instructions, illustrations for constructing handsome, useful pieces, among them a Sheraton desk, Chippendale chair, Spanish desk, Queen Anne table and a William and Mary dressing mirror. 224pp. 8⅛ x 11¼. 29338-6 Pa. $13.95

THE FOSSIL BOOK: A Record of Prehistoric Life, Patricia V. Rich et al. Profusely illustrated definitive guide covers everything from single-celled organisms and dinosaurs to birds and mammals and the interplay between climate and man. Over 1,500 illustrations. 760pp. 7½ x 10⅞. 29371-8 Pa. $29.95

Prices subject to change without notice.

Available at your book dealer or write for free catalog to Dept. GI, Dover Publications, Inc., 31 East 2nd St., Mineola, N.Y. 11501. Dover publishes more than 500 books each year on science, elementary and advanced mathematics, biology, music, art, literary history, social sciences and other areas.